WORDS FROM THE WISE

"I'm a big fan of Chris's approach to innovation. His practical, solutions-oriented (and funny!) strategies for building and exercising innovation muscles are relatable and eminently useful."

—EMILY CHANG, CMO STARBUCKS CHINA

"Chris Denson not only delivers the funny and the creative, but he delivers the absolute truth about what it takes to be an innovator in today's world. He expertly extracts timeless principles from his guests and his own experience and packages them in a way that is entertaining, honest, and inspiring. What's most impressive about Chris is how smoothly shaved his head is. Shine on."

—ORLANDO JONES, ACTOR, COMEDIAN, ENTREPRENEUR

"Want to learn about what makes innovators tick? Look no further than Chris Denson. I was fortunate to be interviewed by Chris. Whether you're a college student or a seasoned entrepreneur, you'll find that the humor, enthusiasm, and inquisitiveness that Chris brings to each interview is as informative as it is entertaining. His book is a must read for all innovators."

—JODI GOLDSTEIN, EXECUTIVE DIRECTOR,
HARVARD INNOVATION LABS

"In today's era of entrepreneurs being modern-day stars, Chris has created a global platform to share the personal secrets to success."

—ROMAN TSUNDER, FOUNDER OF PTTOW/WORLDZ

"Chris Denson is a one-of-a-kind guide through the gardens of innovation who always stops to smell the flowers."

—BARNET BAIN, DIRECTOR OF *MILTON'S SECRET*,
PRODUCER OF *WHAT DREAMS MAY COME*,
AUTHOR OF *THE BOOK OF DOING AND BEING*

"It's about time someone created a show about innovation that is fun and informative. Innovation is inspired in many ways and comes in many forms and from all sorts of people. Chris and his team have created a platform that stealthily stimulates thought and promotes progress. Now you can get it in book form!"

—HAKEEM OLUSEYI, ASTROPHYSICIST, FORMER
CHIEF SCIENCE OFFICER, DISCOVERY NETWORKS

CRUSHING THE BOX

CRUSHING THE BOX

10 ESSENTIAL RULES FOR BREAKING ESSENTIAL RULES

CHRIS DENSON

LIONCREST
PUBLISHING

CRUSHING THE BOX
10 Essential Rules for Breaking Essential Rules

ISBN   978-1-5445-1040-8 *Paperback*
       978-1-5445-1039-2 *Ebook*

CONTENTS

INTRODUCTION

A blinding light shined down on me from somewhere up above. My palms were sweating. My mouth was dry. I felt the pressure deep in my chest. I had to force myself to breathe. All eyes were on me.

There I was, a bright-eyed seventeen-year-old who had just left the nest for the first time in his young life. Now I was standing on a stage in front of hundreds of audience members who were demanding to be entertained. My mission? Make them laugh. No matter what.

Let me back up a bit and tell you how I got on that stage.

My mom was a teacher. She grew up in Detroit's Brewster Projects and married at eighteen. She wouldn't go to college until she was in her thirties and divorced with three kids, and she went on to earn two master's degrees. It's no surprise that by the time I was ten, she had a vision of me as an adult carrying a briefcase and wearing a suit to work. But that's not what I wanted to do with my life.

I wanted to make people laugh.

I always liked jokes. I remember when we used to have the Scholastic book fair, and while other kids were buying *Catcher in the Rye* and young adult novels, I was buying books of knock-knock jokes and reading them in the back seat to my mom. We had this weird duality where she thought I would follow a more traditional path—that is, get a real job—but I had a genuine interest in something else. I'll tell you my story in this introduction because it really is an innovator's journey. I think you'll see why.

THE OPENING ACT

During my freshman year at Michigan State University, there were signs on campus that said, "Wanted: Opening Acts for Cedric the Entertainer." I always loved watching stand-up comedy. Even to this day, it's my primary viewing experience. I thought being the opening act for Cedric the Entertainer would be a great chance to turn something I loved into something I actually did.

I wrote some material, and about a week later, I went to

the audition. A week after that, they called and invited me to be one of the opening acts. I thought, "I guess I'd better learn how to do stand-up for real."

I started performing at the one comedy club in town—Connxtions Comedy Club in Lansing, Michigan. I had about a month before Cedric's show came to town, so I honed my act as much as I could, burning through a litany of bad puns, painful physical performances, and uncomfortable where-are-you-guys-from exchanges with audience members.

Eventually, after a lot of testing and feedback, I settled on my best jokes, and my act was solid. That early experience led me down a six-year-long path of doing stand-up. I won a few comedy competitions, performed on Gilbert Godfrey's *USA Up All Night* show, and wrote jokes alongside my fellow up-and-comers. I hosted a lot of shows on campus and made some television appearances.

Meanwhile, I was earning an engineering degree. Specifically, I studied packaging engineering, which is a rare degree in and of itself. There are only a handful of schools in the United States that offer it. At the time, I figured every company that makes something needs to put it in a package, so I saw it as job security. Nevertheless, it wasn't my passion; I still gravitated toward entertainment.

After graduation, I worked at Chrysler as an engineer for

a couple of years. It was a great job for a recent college graduate, and it was an interesting journey. But working at Chrysler affirmed that I like jokes and entertaining more than I liked engineering.

Almost twenty years later, I'd find a way to combine those two worlds—engineering and humor—through my interview series *Innovation Crush*, which I've always referred to as a cross between *Fast Company* and *The Daily Show*. I get to interview some of the great innovators of our time, people and bands like Nolan Bushnell, Sugar Ray Leonard, Linda Boff, Jean Case, Miguel McKelvey, Troy Carter, OK Go, Cindy Gallop, Arcade Fire, and more.

FIRST TIME ONSTAGE

The first time I got up onstage was both an exhilarating and exhausting experience. I was extremely well rehearsed. Almost overly so. I practiced by recording myself on a tape recorder, then I would listen to my delivery, rewrite the jokes, and do it again a different way. I'd let friends listen to the recordings, run bits past them, and request feedback. Eventually, my act was fully scripted, though I left room for improvisation. I had watched enough stand-up to get a sense of how it should look.

I was also competing in martial arts at the time. I did a joke that involved someone surprise attacking me from behind, followed by a performance of a bunch of karate moves onstage, then apologizing to my grandmother because I didn't know it was her. (I know what you're thinking, but come on, I was seventeen. What else did you expect?) But there I was, fully rehearsed, stretched, and ready to go.

The room I performed in was a bowl-shaped theater that held about five hundred people. I remember standing backstage, looking out at the crowd through the curtain and getting some pretty serious butterflies. After all, this was black comedy, and I don't mean dark comedy. I mean African American comedy, and that's probably the most critical audience you can be in front of. Black audiences can be ruthless, and since this was on a college campus, these were also people I knew. If I bombed, I would still have to see them every day, and you know college kids can be savage AF.

When the emcee called me up, I was on autopilot. Here's how a typical comedy set goes. You introduce yourself and start off slowly. It's not necessarily crickets, but there's a quiet anticipation as you begin your set. You can feel the fact that people are waiting for you to make them laugh. Once you get that first laugh, especially for the first time ever, you feel a sense of relief. Even when you auditioned, they weren't really laughing. They were just watching, with a chuckle here and there. It's hard to perform when someone's jotting down notes in the middle of you pouring your creative heart out. But to finally see an audience genuinely laugh? An audience that isn't even drunk because they're underage? There's no better feeling in the world.

When you're up onstage and the lights are in your face, you can't see the audience. In my novice experience, that was unexpected. If someone heckled me, I wouldn't even know who said it. In order to fire back, I needed to know what the guy was wearing or what he or she looked like. But I wouldn't even be able tell what part of the room it was coming from if it happened. Luckily, it didn't—at least not that time.

The set went great, and I got a lot of laughs. My mind as I exited the stage was a combination of "OMG" and "What just happened?" In the midst of the head rush, I almost missed Cedric's compliments and subsequent handshake. Perhaps most importantly for my then unforeseen future, I learned what it was like to connect with an audience.

Later in my collegiate comedy career, I had a friend who was a telecommunications major and had access to cameras and editing equipment. One night, he suggested we do a sketch comedy show. A short while later, we decided to produce our own sketch show, and we called it *The Nuts*. We went through the whole casting process. I wrote a bunch of sketch scripts, which I had never done before.

We had a casting call on campus and selected the six or seven most talented people to become a part of the cast. A few weeks later, we did a table read, which was even more euphoric for me than stand-up. It was thrilling to watch the room explode in laugh-tears as we went from joke to joke.

The cold open itself was about as good as we could pull off with our limited time, budget, and resources. It went a little something like this: Our director was preparing for a party in his apartment.

"I've got the chips. I've got the soda. What am I forgetting? Pizza? No. The games? Hmmm...ooohhh...the *nuts!*"

Then we—the cast—all burst out from nowhere and got the party started in utterly ridiculous fashion. It was magical to see something that was just a thought only a few weeks before come together and air on MSU's college television station, and eventually end up on a Lansing TV network.

Keep in mind, I had no formal training in either stand-up or television writing. I had never acted, performed, taken a workshop, or so much as read a how-to blog on either craft. This was all heart and passion and gut and blind naïveté. I wrote jokes my way, in my own style, and did whatever felt right at the time. But to see it pay off time and time again was incredible.

After that first table read, I felt so euphoric that I went and bought a cigar. Still wet behind the ears, I had never smoked or drank alcohol, believe it or not. In fact, I wouldn't even have my first drink until my twenty-first birthday. Nevertheless, I went and had a cigar on the porch of my apartment building to celebrate because I thought, "This is it." I had never felt as emotionally connected to anything I had ever done. To this day, I refer to that experience as a "goosebump moment." You'll read more about the importance of goosebump moments later in this book.

I ended up doing stand-up comedy for the next six years. It's what I was passionate about. All through school, I was earning an engineering degree that I didn't care about. I mean, I cared about it in the way that you care about a well-crafted pair of counterfeit Air Jordans. Sure, they look good, and everyone's impressed. But deep down inside, you know you're wearing fake sneakers, and you don't plan on keeping them for long. So even though I took my engineering studies seriously, I knew in my heart that I was only passionate about two things: comedy and martial arts.

Stand-up was the first activity that I truly loved doing. It was an expression of who I was, combining an untapped passion I had for entertaining people with the immediate feedback for putting myself and my creative work out there. Audiences accepted it. My friends accepted it. People saw me as a comedian, and it validated my unique combination of writing skill and personal creativity.

THE SAME OLD JOKES

Despite my love of the craft, I ultimately left stand-up behind after six years. Telling the same jokes and performing the same five- or twenty-minute routine over and over felt like being a hamster on a wheel. As much as I liked performing for an audience, I sensed there must be something more to this comedy business. Once I started writing comedy, I knew I'd found my real passion. Stand-up was repetitious, the same set of jokes night after night, and I thrived on spontaneity and creativity.

I craved constant creation, and writing allowed me to create something, leave it there, and move on to the next new idea. Also, I didn't want to be a starving road comic, doing fifty-dollar gigs in a different city every night. But the two went hand in hand. Stand-up was a great platform for immediate feedback and validation, and writing was a place to imagine creating any world where anything could happen. I continued doing both, even after I graduated and took that briefcase to work at Chrysler's headquarters in Auburn Hills, Michigan.

One of my best friends from college, a musician, had

been living in Los Angeles for a year, and we would talk about the things he'd seen, the people he'd met, and how awesome the West Coast was treating him. Eventually, he invited me to come check it out for a week. Wanting to capitalize on my time there, I sent at least fifty writing samples to various studios in Hollywood. This was preinternet internet, and email wasn't popping like it is today, so I bought one of those Hollywood directories online for twenty bucks.

"Oh boy! Hollywood is gonna love me!" I thought as I attached my cover letter to packet after packet of sketches I wrote and put in the mail. One of those sketches was entitled "B.E.T. the Black Extra-Terrestrial." It explored the concept of E.T. landing in Compton rather than Tujunga. You can do the math on how that turned out for E.T.

Hollywood loved my letters, all right. I arrived in LA on a Sunday, fully prepped for the one meeting I managed to set up coming on Thursday. The meeting went well.

The woman, a development executive who either thought I was amazing or felt pity for me, asked, "Who else have you met with?"

When I told her that I hadn't met with anyone, she made a bunch of phone calls right then and there, and I had three meetings the next day.

One of them was with a person in development at Fox who suggested I should come back to Hollywood during pilot season and to make sure I contacted him when I did. That was all I needed to hear. In my mind, I was Calvin from those old McDonald's commercials from the 1990s. You might remember, Calvin's job at Mickey D's made him the hottest kid in the neighborhood. "Did you hear? Calvin owns McDonald's!"

My mind was made up. I went back to Michigan and packed my bags for California. I drove thirty-six hours straight from my mom's door to my studio apartment in Hollywood. By the way, if you've ever been to the actual city of Hollywood, you probably feel bad for this younger me. Let's just say it's not exactly Beverly Hills.

To this day, I've never seen or heard from that Fox executive again. Not that I was necessarily banking on that one opportunity at Fox; I was just excited that someone had expressed interest in me. I took it as a sign, but it ultimately turned into a stop sign because the guy got my hopes up and then disappeared on me. Welcome to Hollywood!

After that, I tried to keep the momentum going. I had three months of savings in the bank and did whatever I could to get by. I worked as a personal trainer for a little while and did a couple of odd jobs, and after a few months, I wound up as a production assistant on *The Leeza Gibbons Show.* By the eighth month, I got a writing job with BET for their first attempt at late night, *Live from L.A.* I'm sure it was because of my beautifully crafted E.T.-meets-Jheri-curl-alien sketch. John Salley and another comedian named Michael Colyar hosted the show. It was fun because I got to create, write, and act. Every night was new.

I met some great people and formed relationships that would help me later in my career. I wrote with one of the guys who created *America's Next Top Model* and *Blackish* and wrote the movie *Girls Trip.* Another guy on that show had worked with the Wayans family since their *In Living Color* days. Another writer sold a script to Oprah. It was a really solid crew, and many of them are still my friends to this day.

Then I learned another hard lesson. Coming from the Midwest, even working at Chrysler, I was used to the idea that you get plenty of notice if a company decides to terminate your employment. One day we went in to collect our paychecks, and there was a letter stapled to the outside of the envelope: "Don't come in on Monday." All of the writing staff was let go. No advance notice. The shock was something similar to standing in a circle of friends at a party, having a gay old time, and getting a text message that reads "I'm pregnant" from a number you don't have saved in your phone.

That was a shock for me. I was twenty-two, and they fired us all with no warning. I didn't even know they could do that. Lesson learned. I started taking a lot of odd jobs to make sure I had income. I worked in events. I promoted night clubs. I met another friend who was a music video producer, so I worked on music videos as an associate producer. I performed comedy at events. I even got a real estate license. I did whatever job I could get my hands on because I didn't want to be caught off guard again. I started developing a broader cultural curiosity as a result.

At one point, I worked twice a year at MAGIC, a fashion conference in Las Vegas. Prior to that, I didn't even know they had fashion conferences. It was fun being in an environment around other types of creative people. I maintained a cadence of projects. When you work in the entertainment industry, you go from project to project, so everything is a new start, and everything is a clean slate. I liked that. Each project was an opportunity to invent from scratch. On the other hand, constantly looking for the next job was exhausting.

NEW LIFE

During that time, I became a dad for the first time. Before I knew it, I had gone from popping bottles to filling them with baby formula. About a year after the birth of my daughter, I became a single dad. Her mom moved out of state, so I was a full-time single dad with a beautiful baby girl. That shifted my priorities. For the sake of being a parent, I decided I needed consistent, reliable work rather than a stream of freelance jobs that could end at any time.

I took a full-time job as the first marketing director for the New York Film Academy in Los Angeles. I knew the entertainment side of the business, and I knew marketing because I had some sort of creative input on how to better reach the audience in a lot of the projects I worked on. I was sort of a natural at marketing.

The New York Film Academy had never had a marketing director before, so it was a totally blank canvas, and that blank-canvas theme has become a thread throughout my career. There was no formula. I made it up as I went along.

Luckily, I had a couple of big hits right out of the gate. For starters, Facebook was the new kid on the block, and though it still required a .edu email address to join, it was kicking Myspace in the teeth and signing up new members by the thousands. Guess what has two thumbs and created the New York Film Academy's Facebook page? I was producing photoshoots near the Hollywood sign, building out social media, and brokering partnerships with film festivals. We even did a partnership with *America's Next Top Model* where the contestants came to the New York Film Academy for an episode to learn acting, stage presence, taking direction, connecting with character, and how to move on set. Although not huge industry firsts, these were definitely firsts for the New York Film Academy, and there was definitely no shortage of blank canvases out there to paint on.

After a while, I gravitated from the New York Film Academy to the American Film Institute, where they had a digital content lab. The digital content lab was basically a think tank for creatives. Four of us ran the lab, and we recruited some of the smartest and most creative people in the world. I met Nolan Bushnell there. I met Bill Duke. I met all of these incredible creators. We did work with the Leonardo DiCaprio Foundation. We built the first in-browser game for the PlayStation. We were funded by the Corporation for Public Broadcasting, Adobe, and Intel. As one of the most sought-after labs in the country, there was no shortage of future-forward technologists, builders, thinkers, and doers volunteering their time and resources to help us create the future.

What I liked most of all was that we created for the sake of creating. We would think of a concept and—as long as it had some long-term industry implication—build it out in just a matter of weeks. I realized that what I was truly passionate about wasn't necessarily writing jokes or doing stand-up comedy, but something much broader. It was creating—thinking up something really cool and then bringing it to life. I had a passion for it, and I was good at it.

THE JOY OF INNOVATING

I had this sense of wonder about everything I experienced during my time at AFI. I was a catalyst for creating new ideas and bringing them to life, watching people take risks on brand-new platforms, or creating new ones all together. We all had a desire to creatively express ourselves, to develop ideas nobody had ever seen before, and to make them happen. Our job at the lab was to make sure that we were predictors and creators of the future.

I've never been a fan of formula. It's one of the reasons I left Chrysler. It was often the same set of problems with the same set of solutions. It seemed to me like they talked about the same problems for years. "How can we do a better job of shipping transmissions?"

After they were working on the same problems for so long, I thought, "How come that hasn't been solved yet?" I felt like many of the employees were there because of tenure or for their pension, so they weren't trying too hard to reinvent anything. They were biding their time until retirement. It was just a different mindset about what it means to be creative.

In contrast, I was entering circles in Los Angeles that I never thought I would be in. I worked in this constant state of creation to the point that, for a few years, I didn't know where I belonged. Did I want to do stand-up comedy? Did I want to be a TV writer? Did I want to be an innovator? Did I want to be a marketer? Maybe I wanted to have my own company since I was doing all of those different jobs simultaneously. But there was something I knew that was valuable about all of these creative skills coming together.

When I hire for innovation teams today, the type of misfit toys I look for are oddball polymaths who have experimented in many areas of business and creativity. There's an innate cultural curiosity in all of us, despite specific skills or careers that might define us. Plus, when you're creating or inventing or reimagining, you're looking under all kinds of rocks and having unique experiences.

For instance, one of the guys on my team for *Innovation Crush* studied religion, was a DJ, worked for a few years as a copywriter, lived in Japan for three years working in medical research, and now takes all that cultural experience and brings together different ideas, ideals, and resources for many of the projects we work on. At OMD, which is considered to be the world's largest media agency, many of my team members don't have any media experience at all.

Sounds great on the surface, but of course, every coin

has two sides. Except for bitcoins. I think bitcoins have zero sides. Or an infinite amount of sides? That question is one for the cryptosages.

Anyway, at one point in my career, knowing I was a bit of a misfit, I took almost an entire year off to be sure I made the right career move that would allow me to express all my different sides. I had a lot of general meetings with start-ups, big corporations, agencies, and everyone in between. I softly explained to them my place and purpose in this world, which was mainly to be a catalyst to innovation. The conversation was always the same.

"Oh, wait, so you're a creative director."

"Yeah," I would reply, "but not really."

"Oh, so you're a strategist."

"Kind of."

"Oh, you're the technology guy."

"Well, that's part of what I do."

"So you're funny, and you can write?"

"Well, yes, that, too, but..."

I remember thinking, "I'm all of those things." I'm the guy who can connect the dots where you may not normally connect them. That talent for dot-connecting grew out of all of the experiences I had in my career early on. At the end of the day, it was all storytelling. Either it was telling the story of our lives via social media, pitching an idea, or even telling a story in the literal, literary sense.

There were several periods in my career where I felt like I was on a desert island. It felt like nobody understood my point of view or saw the world the way I saw it. However, the one idea that was universally binding was the idea of marketing. Oh yeah. Every individual and every corporation are searching for ways to cut through the clutter and get people excited enough about their message, product, service, or skills.

I don't care who you are; if you're going to a job interview, you're a marketer at that point. You're marketing who you are as an individual. Your résumé is marketing collateral. Your LinkedIn profile is marketing. That stupid selfie you took at Coachella with Drake on stage in the background? That's marketing. Even if you're the CEO of a Fortune 500 company speaking at the annual all-hands meeting (shout-out to cold Costco croissants), you're marketing the idea that your company is awesome and that people shouldn't go work for the guys with the warm croissants.

Let's say you have an idea to create a VR experience that combines scents and real-life roller skates? At some point, you need to convince someone—an investor, the roller-skating company, your grandma—that it's a worthy idea. First of all, good luck with that, weirdo. Second, you're still marketing.

SIMILARITIES TO STAND-UP COMEDY

I credit my success in innovation, at least in part, to my background in stand-up comedy. Some of my best ideas often start from jokes. Specifically puns. I say something silly and ridiculous and then realize, "Actually, this does kind of make sense." Then when I write and deliver a joke, it has to be translatable to a mass of people. It may not work. There have been tons of my jokes that have bombed. You've listened to the show, right? As a comedian, you have to present your ideas in a way that the most people can understand. Your job is to translate your own observations into original creativity.

Stand-up is a solo game. You're up there by yourself. Similarly, the innovator's journey is often a lonely one. You've created something, or you have an idea, and you're the only person who sees it the way you see it. There's just you. Then you go test the idea with a friend or a coworker. Then you refine it. Then you find a bigger audience. Some respond the way you had hoped; others don't. Refine again.

Test again. Build. Perform. Repeat. The whole time, you act with the same energy and excitement you had when it was just a nugget of an idea.

Just like doing a comedy set—which is basically pitching ideas and thoughts to an audience—the bright light is staring you in the face, and everybody's waiting for you to impress them. You don't know if they've had a bad day or an awesome one. You don't know if they heard a million and one jokes just like this or if you are the unicorn of funny, spewing a rainbow of laughs. You must believe in what you're talking about. It's not just telling jokes that you think are smart and scientifically clever (though you should do that, too), but telling jokes that you genuinely believe in and have a passion for—even when it doesn't go well.

If you're an entrepreneur and you're pitching your business to a bunch of investors, you'll more than likely hear no a lot more than you will hear yes. You're going to feel like you're bombing more often than not. The good news is, the more you put yourself out there, the more resilient you become to the downside. One no is not necessarily a rejection of you or your idea. Pitching requires persistence; you have to keep pitching until you find the right receptive audience. It's just like that creepy guy with the oversized blazer hitting on women at the club. That dude's like, "Not interested? OK." And he just accepts it and moves on to the next one. Like, literally the one next to the one who just shot him down. It's all a disgusting numbers game until someone says yes.

Of course, no matter how persistent you are, it's essential in any endeavor to consider the feedback you're receiving. In writing there's a saying, "Writing is rewriting." In other words, revising and incorporating feedback is an essential part of the process. This concept is especially important in any creative profession.

Ask any musician about a song they perform, and very rarely will they tell you that the finished result is exactly the same as when they first thought of it. Music producers, backup singers, and audio engineers all add a little something to the mix. An opinion. A riff. A new idea a week later. After enough people collaborate, pretty soon, you have a hit song.

In any creative profession, you begin to learn how to filter through feedback, incorporate what you agree with, and do away with what you don't. For me as a writer, sometimes the joke was funny in my head, but not so much when I wrote it on paper and said it out loud to the rest of the group. So you rewrite it. But then a producer or another writer hears the revised joke and points out that the character already said a similar joke earlier. So you rewrite it again. Then the talent says the joke during the table read, and it doesn't come off the way you thought it would because the timing was off or the setup took too long. You rewrite it again. You might even start over with a page-one rewrite on a script, which means starting from scratch but still incorporating the feedback you received along the way. That is what we call the creative process. Creativity is truly a team effort.

INSIGHTS FROM STAND-UP

I never thought that stand-up would be a metaphor for life. But it is. So much goes into crafting a joke, putting yourself out there, connecting with an audience, reading their feedback, and risking humiliation. You can bomb five nights in a row, and that sixth night, you're the king of the world. That sixth night is the beacon. You're holding on to that little bit of hope that it'll all turn around, and that reenergizing boost is all you needed to keep going. I think every entrepreneur has been there, whether you've failed multiple times, you're currently failing, or you can't figure out how to take the first step.

As you begin to succeed, you will evolve. As you reach a level of success, now you want to strive for an even higher level of success. Success begets more success. Often this has more to do with the habit of putting yourself out there than perfecting the creative craft.

In the documentary *Dying Laughing* almost every comic

in the film says their career turned around after they decided to be themselves. They were doing OK when they were trying to mimic other successful comedians or just doing jokes, but once they started telling personal stories about their wife or their kids or the time they got arrested or battled depression, they began to achieve much greater success. The real-life experiences that they thought were mundane powerfully revealed who they were as individuals, and that allowed them to connect with the audience. The same is true in innovation. I've seen it come out time and time again in the conversations I've had on *Innovation Crush* in which someone's incredibly personal experience is leveraged to create amazing ideas that the world identifies with.

Through stand-up, I got in the habit of looking at the parallels in life. When you become culturally curious, you start to see similarities in art, fashion, medicine, education, and how people react to stimuli. Where do the endorphins kick in? What do we all want as human beings? What do we as creators want to give people? How do we fulfill that need in a moment? Or for a lifetime? These are all powerful questions that every creative person must wrestle with.

ABOUT THIS BOOK

This book is about innovation and helping readers find or increase their true potential as creatives and innovators.

As the host of *Innovation Crush*, I've met some of the most intriguing thought leaders and innovators in the world. With every interview, I learned something new. It is those key nuggets of information that I am sharing in this book.

I'm not only an interviewer; I'm also a practitioner. Many of the stories you'll read in the following chapters come from my own experiences as well. That dual role—as both interviewer and innovator—gives me a unique perspective on the innovation process and the nature of creativity. I'm simultaneously an outsider and an insider, a student and a teacher.

This book will introduce ten unexpected metaphors for how to harness creativity and create something unique and useful. I promise not to bore you with academic rigor, pie charts, and tons of technical jargon. My goal is to inspire us all to believe in the power of creativity and ideas and follow our own innovative paths, no matter how unusual or circuitous the route may be. Whatever your background, no matter where you're coming from or how successful you are, if you're fascinated by innovation and creating, you've come to the right place.

SWIM LIKE AN OTTER

When you think of the people who work at NASA's Jet Propulsion Lab, where they design vehicles for space travel, you probably assume they're all rocket scientists, computer programmers, aerospace engineers, or Matt Damon from that movie *The Martian*. You'll find most of them there. But you certainly wouldn't expect to find any artists at NASA, right?

One of the most fascinating guests on *Innovation Crush* is a guy named Dan Goods. Dan works at NASA, but he's not a scientist or a mathematician. He's NASA's artist-in-residence and chief visual strategist. In that role, Dan helps the space agency develop public art exhibitions that showcase and explain scientific concepts. The theory is that scientists and engineers are great at building stuff, but they sometimes need a little help communicating complex scientific theories to the general public. That's where Dan comes in.

Dan studied visual arts at the Art Center College of Design where he graduated as valedictorian of his class. Today, Dan's creative work is seen in public spaces, art museums, and even outer space. He's worked on the famous eCLOUD project, which is a 108-foot, data-driven sculpture that responds to weather around the world. Google it. Or better yet, YouTube it.

He was also a driving force behind an exhibit titled Metamorphosis. It allowed visitors to experience the atmosphere of a comet. He's currently developing the Museum of Awe, which I'm willing to bet will be awe-some!

Dan impressed me with plenty of fascinating stories when he appeared on *Innovation Crush*, but one in particular stands out. Dan learned to swim like an otter. Yup, you read that right. When he was an art student, he was given an assignment to draw a picture of a sea otter. But rather than Googling a few images of sea otters or watching YouTube videos, his teacher wanted Dan to go deeper to really understand the nature of sea otters. But how?

First, Dan had to go find real, living sea otters and observe how they behave. What are their habits? What do they eat? What eats them? How do they play with other sea otters?

That wasn't too difficult—almost all zoos and aquariums have sea otters. Plus, I hear they're delicious.

Dan watched the cute little mammals frolic and swim around. But that wasn't enough. Part of the assignment was to pay special attention to the body mechanics of how otters swim. The art teacher wanted Dan to immerse himself in the sea otters' world...literally.

So Dan got out his swim trunks and dove in. To understand the sea otters' world, the art teacher insisted that the students fully immerse themselves in the life of a sea otter. And it worked. After struggling to mimic the body mechanics of the animals, Dan began to understand why they're built the way they are, how important webbed feet are for marine propulsion, why a tail is helpful for balance, and how important fur is to create a natural layer of insulation against the cold water.

This unusual exercise helped Dan learn one of the most valuable skills any innovator can have: empathy. He actually learned the value of putting himself into the world of his subject. Only then could he truly empathize with the subject's needs, wants, challenges, and lifestyle.

OTTERLY IMMERSE YOURSELF

In any creative endeavor, such as launching a business,

doing a marketing project, or building something from scratch, it's crucial to immerse yourself in the culture so you can build empathy. Just as Dan dove into the water to better understand the environment of sea otters, businesspeople and creatives need to dive in to the culture of their audience. The goal is to fully experience what that audience perceives. Not just to read about it, but to actually dive in and experience it firsthand.

This immersion technique goes far beyond what most businesspeople, marketers, and creative types do when, for example, launching a new product. The typical process involves collecting market data, studying demographics, doing a few focus groups, and researching online. All of that stuff is important, but it leaves out a critical piece: the experience.

Imagine a start-up company that wants to launch a new product to sell to fans at NASCAR races. They can study the demographics, watch NASCAR on TV, rent *Talladega Nights* (shout-out to Mike Honcho) on Amazon Prime, and do focus groups about what NASCAR fans like or dislike. But they won't truly understand the NASCAR mentality until they actually go to a race, sit in the stands, walk the midway, ride in a golf cart through the infield, and spend the weekend in an RV barbecuing chicken wings and drinking Pabst Blue Ribbon. They also need to wait in line for hours to get an autograph from a driver, listen to the pit crews on radio headsets, and sit in a four-hour traffic jam after the race. It's all part of the experience. It's swimming with the otters. There is no way to truly understand and empathize with NASCAR fans by studying spreadsheets, crunching data, reading NASCAR race results online, and interviewing people in a conference room.

You have to experience it.

A FISH OUT OF WATER IS A GOOD THING

One of my favorite thoughts about us as individuals is noting how transferable many of our skills are. For example, a doctor who is great at conversing and empathizing with frightened patients could kill at managing the needs and nuanced demands of a million-dollar marketing client who's concerned about their brand. An accountant working in the food and beverage industry could transfer to a totally different industry—such as advertising, consumer products, or automotive, for example—and bring her reengineering of business finance to the reengineering of corporate operations. Almost out of necessity, I've had to prove that over and over in my career. But what I've learned is that every time you take on a new field, immersion strategy and empathy-building become important once again.

I'm not a video gamer. I'm familiar with them, of course,

but I never really understood the culture. This could have been a problem when I took on a new role as head of creative solutions at a company called Machinima. Machinima is a global content company focused on video games that distributes programming through YouTube, Facebook, Twitter, and other platforms. Not only that, they were first in the space, and by the time I came on board, they were doing billions of views per month.

They brought me in despite the fact that I was not a die-hard gamer. In fact, I didn't play them at all. I didn't know the titles, the jargon, the famous people in that world, and most importantly, I didn't know the culture. But I knew I had to learn about all that stuff, and fast.

So what did I do? I swam with the otters. I snapped on my neon orange Speedo and jumped in the water. I was determined to take a crash course in all things gaming. Of course, I studied the metrics and demographics of the industry. Which is useful. But I knew I needed to immerse myself. It didn't help that many of the employees had been there since day one and were super passionate about their product; they viewed me as an outsider, not a part of their community. They expressed their concerns in that regard more than a few times.

Rather than being the guy walking in with all the answers, my first strategy was to just shut up and listen. I observed everything and talked to everyone I could at Machinima. I asked a lot of questions. I became genuinely curious about gaming. I visited every different department in the company and tried to figure out what they were passionate about. I listened not only from a business perspective, but also from pure curiosity. I was genuinely curious about the passion these people had.

The next thing I did was make the decision to not just be an observer, but also a participant. I started learning the jargon and terminology, like MMORPG, PWNing, FPS, or even oddball YouTube comments like "First!" I watched countless hours of videos of people making gaming videos. I also learned that many of these influencers have more followers—and money—than traditional Hollywood celebrities. I studied everything within the fanboy universe: animation, EDM, Star Wars, Harry Potter, *The Big Bang Theory*, tournaments, teams, and content creators. It was a deep dive into influencer culture.

Then I went to VidCon and Comic-Con in San Diego and witnessed passion for the industry on a whole new level. I remember seeing a literal stampede of fans running down a convention hallway to try to meet their favorite gamer who was surrounded by six security guards. I watched as another famous player stood on his hotel balcony and interacted with a mob of hundreds of fanboys and girls below. It was an eye-opening experience, to say the least. I immersed myself with superfans and superstars. I attended all the panel discussions, stood in line to get autographs, and went to parties where talent and industry experts would gather with fans. The funny thing about immersion is that whatever you're experiencing during the immersion sticks with you. To this day, I still go to Comic-Con or E3 or PAX out of pure joy of participating in the industry and observing how it operates.

My immersion into the world was eye opening—and fun. But most of all, it changed my perception of the industry and the people who love it. I admit that before Machinima, I held some negative beliefs about gamers. That's probably because we live in a headline-driven society: we read a few stories in the news or on social media, and we assume that we understand something. But those perceptions are often wrong. Like most of us, I thought most gamers were pimply faced, antisocial geeks who lived in their parents' basement. But the more I immersed myself, the deeper I went—and the more I embraced the community—the more my eyes were opened. I met plenty of young men and women who went from rags to riches through their elevated level of play. They became millionaires and now have influence with millions of followers around the world.

I realized that this tightly knit community encompasses people from all walks of life—from executives to professionals to doctors to PhD grad students. They come in all colors, shapes, sizes, and ages. For fun, I highly recommend you Google the Granny Gamer. I learned that there is a level of sophistication in this community that I never knew existed. They have their own language, customs, etiquette, and subcommunities. I learned volumes about this industry and the people in it that I never would have been exposed to by sitting in front of my office computer screen, perusing industry statistics and studying spreadsheets.

Making the effort to immerse myself made all the difference.

BEEN THERE, DONE THAT

After a business reaches a critical mass in the marketplace, a certain size, or a certain comfort level, there is a time when complacency might set in. After establishing a secure place in the market, the level of closeness to the audience or the customers begins to slip. Marketing teams assume they understand the customer, so they stop trying to connect with them in new and innovative ways.

This disconnect from customers happens gradually, so it often goes unnoticed. After so many years of being an established brand, companies tend to use the same marketing channels year after year. It's an easy trap to fall into. Take a TV series for instance: it's the same audience watching the same program on the same day at the same time. We got 'em. They're not going anywhere. When it comes to understanding their customers, they think, "Focus groups, market research…been there done that. We know who our customers are. No need to keep researching them." That is, until that new show comes out on the other channel and starts to steal audience share. Then there's a mad scramble to do something creative and clever to get the viewers back.

It's sort of a been-there-done-that mentality. It's dangerous. Companies that are chugging along and succeeding in the marketplace tend to assume they already know all they need to know about their audience. They stop trying to learn about their customers. Instead, they stick to their tried and true methods of reaching those customers. "We've always done direct mail advertising, and it works fine, so let's keep doing it." Whatever has worked before, they think it will keep working. Rinse and repeat.

For example, if an automobile dealership group has spent the last decade marketing to customers through local television ads, that's probably what they will tend to do in the future. There's a comfort level they have with doing the same routine that they've always done. But many of their customers have radically changed how they consume media and advertising, let alone how they interact with friends or family, or even how the traditional idea of what a family is has changed. The dealer group risks losing touch with their customers' evolving needs and lifestyles. The been-there-done-that strategy doesn't lead to prosperity and growth—it leads to stagnation.

At one point in my career, I was developing creative marketing strategies for a large and very successful financial institution. We went to work creating the most engaging campaigns—campaigns that were more innovative than anything the bank had done before. Time and time again, I thought, "Now *this* is the one!"

I was wrong. The bank shot down every idea we had. Turns out that their appetite for creative risks was lower than what they even thought it was.

"We don't necessarily need to be clever," they decided. "We need to make people feel safe and familiar." Despite being thoroughly impressed with our thinking, they passed on all of the ideas put before them and decided to keep doing many of the things they had been doing that got them to where they were.

Established brands seldom want to rock the boat. They think what they've always done is working well enough, so they hesitate to innovate. Even young companies run the same risks. While being safe is smart, the opposite can sometimes be fatal. Take Blockbuster Video for example. They failed to innovate by sticking to their tried-and-true, brick-and-mortar business despite impending indications of a cultural shift to more digital interactions. Their refusal to innovate eventually bankrupted the company. (We'll talk more about Blockbuster in chapter 2.)

BE THERE, DO THAT

When it comes to understanding your customers, the best way to avoid the pitfalls of the been-there-done-that mentality is to replace it with a be-there-do-that mentality. You stay in tune and connected by diving in and swimming with the sea otters. Go live in their world for a while. Go to that NASCAR race. Attend the conventions where your target customers will be. Show up at their events. Go to their school. Tailgate at a football game with them. Seek them out and spend time with them. Ask them every question you can think of. Understand what they're passionate about and why.

I learned this lesson when I was working at the American Film Institute's Digital Content Lab. We were developing a program with the Vans Warped Tour involving high school students. We were asking teens to bring in their old cellphones and accessories to an AT&T dealer in exchange for points toward Warped Tour tickets and merchandise, and even a chance to meet some of the performers. After we had already designed the promotion, we thought, "Well, maybe we should go talk to some high school kids to see what they think of this program?"

We visited a high school and talked to a bunch of teens in the target market, and we filmed it. Wow, was that an eye-opener. Many of the assumptions we made about high school students were flat-out wrong. From what kind of data plans they had to who owned their phones to whose plan they were on to how often they were even using their phones, we got it wrong. The promotion would have been a flop because we misunderstood our audience. Based on what we learned by physically going into their environment and spending time with them, we revamped the promotion—and it worked.

The least effective idea is to sit in an office, review data, read articles, and study research reports about your target market, then mistakenly assume you know who they are. That's not immersion—that's lazy. Staying in tune with customers in an ever-changing world with proliferating technology and marketing channels takes real effort.

Anything you can do while sitting in your office is what I call "observing and translating." It doesn't work. You need to replace observing and translating with immersing and translating. You have to leave your comfort zone and dive into your customer's comfort zone. Look, feel, touch, and experience their world firsthand.

Innovators physically put themselves in the shoes—or swim fins, wetsuit, bicycle, or game console—of their audience. In order to really jumpstart creativity and inspiration, get out there and swim with the sea otters.

Here's a great example of the power of empathy. Music mogul, investor, Atom Factory CEO, and all-around nice guy Troy Carter is perhaps most notably known as Lady Gaga's former manager, credited with taking her from dive bars to superstardom. Along the way, he began to manage several other talents, from Meghan Trainor to Miguel. He later turned his ability to pick winners in entertainment to picking winners in business. He's invested in a bunch of successful start-ups, including Dropbox, Spotify, Warby Parker, Uber, WeTransfer, and others.

Troy appeared on *Innovation Crush*, and when asked what his superpower is, he started to riff on empathy. He has an insane skill for understanding what artists want and need and translating that into opportunity. Being entrepreneurial, he also understood that the grit, passion, and emotional journey of a founder is similar to that of an artist. Troy's been there, done that. As good as he is at spotting musical talent, he's equally adept at spotting start-ups that have the potential to attract an impassioned following. Not a bad skill to have. In fact, we titled the episode "An Empire Built on Empathy."

EAT YOUR BRAIN

One of the more interesting projects I was able to lead involved combining two seemingly unrelated worlds in an unexpected way. It began with a neural mapping company and a production house and ended up as an interactive experience at South by Southwest (SXSW). It was like a clever science fair project in grade school, except this time with zombies.

Zombies are one of the biggest phenomena in popular media. People love zombies; they're everywhere. Hell, how many times does Milla Jovovich need to be called into action to take down the evil Umbrella Corporation? TV shows like *The Walking Dead*, movies like *World War Z*, or my personal favorite, *Train to Busan*, have us all wondering, "Well, what will I do when the zombie apocalypse comes?"

We came up with the idea to partner a medical device company called Emotiv with a new TV series on the CW Network called *iZombie*. The idea was that zombies eat brains, so we thought of a way to demonstrate visually and figuratively why that might be and how it would look.

Emotiv makes a medical-grade device for consumers that monitors brain activity and then displays a full-color image of the active parts of the brain on a screen. Different colors indicated which brainwaves are most active at any given moment, including alpha, beta, delta, theta. Knowing which brainwaves are most active, Emotiv could be prescriptive about the types of activities and tasks that can help you do things like achieve Zen or increase performance. It's a really cool technology that seemed like it would fit perfectly with the brain-eating undead on *iZombie*.

We designed an experience at SXSW where anyone could put on the Emotiv headset and see a live image of their brain activity displayed on a large high-resolution monitor. We also 3D printed brain-shaped candy with color-coding that corresponded with each type of brainwave. For fun, we assigned a fictional flavor profile to each: alpha was sweet, beta was tangy, and so on. Essentially, each participant could eat their own brain.

During the three-hour event, hundreds of people lined

up, and even more stood by and observed. Even the cast members of *iZombie* came through and tried it out. As an added bonus, each individual brain scan was sharable. We could export a digital card with the image of each brain and send it to the person's cell phone, which they could post and share on social media.

BE YOUR OWN SCIENCE EXPERIMENT

We received a lot of buzz at SXSW on that brain "scandy" project. Everyone wanted to stop by, get their head scanned, and eat their own brain. It was a different way to combine different technologies with pop culture to create a memorable brand experience.

More importantly, however, was that this came at a time when wearable technology was beginning to take off. If we could map brainwaves with a simple headset as a novelty marketing experience, just imagine what we could do for any brand. Every brand makes an emotional promise. Snickers, "Really satisfies." Wells Fargo, "Done." Geico, "It was so easy, even a caveman could do it." We would be able to accurately measure the emotional reaction to any movie screening, taste test, thrill ride, or brand message and come up with newfangled ways to connect products and services with customers.

At first, the thought of this experiment was met with

excitement. But it was quickly followed by skepticism. Emotiv viewed themselves as a studied medical application, not as a pop culture novelty. The CW wondered if people would participate in public brain scans and if the start-up had the resources and understanding to drive viewership to a new series. It seemed a little off brand and a little left field to both parties.

Yet that's exactly why we wanted to do it.

Each party had to be convinced of the value of taking risks and testing new ideas. For Emotiv, it was an opportunity to get their product in the hands of a whole new consumer base. For the CW, it was something that would cut through the clutter. For my team, it was a backdoor entry point to a bigger picture.

We knew this was a goosebump idea—one of those ideas that instantly stands out from all the rest. "That's a decent idea. That's an OK idea. But that idea just gave me goosebumps!" It was one of those ideas that makes you tick as an innovator. (We'll talk more about goosebump ideas in chapter 8.)

I know that eating your own brain may feel a little out of left field. It is. You should've seen some of the other ideas that didn't make it! But that's kind of the point. If you want to get to the next level in business or in anything else, go to the extreme in trying something new. If you don't push yourself for uncomfortable, moonshot ideas, then you run the risk of doing the same things that have always been done. During brainstorming sessions, make sure no idea is shut down and nothing is off limits. Expand the minds and boundaries of everyone in the brainstorming session.

One of my mantras is "What got you here won't get you there." In other words, what you've been doing up to this point is enough to have gotten you to where you are, but to rise up to the next level, try something different. It takes new stimuli, insights, inputs, and people to connect with. Be adventurous. Be fun, playful, even childlike. Embrace a spirit of curiosity and experimentation until you come up with that next goosebump idea you just can't get out of your head.

Look for those goosebump ideas, then run with them as far as you can. We all owe it to ourselves to embrace a spirit of childlike adventure and experimentation. Or as this section's heading suggests, be your own science experiment. Mix together those two elements that no one has ever combined before. Don't come up with copycat ideas. Be original. Find what has never been done and do it.

BE A MAD SCIENTIST

Someone who represents this approach to innovation

is Andy Walshe, who was also one of my guests on the *Innovation Crush* podcast. Andy formerly ran Red Bull's High Performance Program.

As you probably know, Red Bull sponsors dozens of extreme athletes. But they also support creatives, including filmmakers, musicians, artists, and performers. Andy was instrumental in helping them reach their peak performance, and he does it by developing social and scientific experiments that resemble what a mad scientist might do.

For example, in an effort to see what the human body is capable of, Andy devised a unique experiment. He knew that a key limiting factor in athlete performance was muscle and aerobic exhaustion. After a period of intense exertion, lactic acid builds up in the muscles and the body feels fatigue. Andy, mad scientist that he is, wondered how much of performance was due to physical limitations versus mental ones.

He placed a specially designed node on the back of the athletes' skulls that turned off the part of the brain that signals fatigue. He wanted to test how much of the typical fatigue response was physiological versus psychological. In other words, if doubt wasn't a factor, how long could the human body persist in a given athletic activity? For me, I'd rather turn off that part of the brain that hears my kids whining. But for Andy, it's about pushing the limits and breaking the boundaries of human performance.

In a different experiment, he wanted to test the power of the athletes' minds to limit their own bodies' performance. He set up an LED light display that ran around the inner rail of an indoor cycling velodrome. The cyclists were asked to match their fastest times ever, and he synchronized the lights to lead the cyclists around the track at the exact same pace.

Andy had the cyclists come back multiple times, and each time, he told them he wanted them to keep pace with the lights, which would be the same as their previous time. Again and again, the athletes were able to sustain their performance. But there was a secret. Little did the athletes know, Andy had sped up the lights. In the athletes' minds, they were doing exactly what they had done before, so they were able to keep pace with the lights. When Andy told them later that their performance was 10 percent faster than before, they were stunned.

Andy's diabolical little science experiment proved that many of the limits of human performance are all in the mind. Sometimes we limit our own capabilities to perform at a higher level. This doesn't only apply to athletes. It applies to any human in any endeavor, including business, the arts, education, sports, and a myriad of other activities where human perception is a limiting factor.

CREATE A CULTURE OF EXPERIMENTATION

Most of us do not have the resources of Red Bull. We can't hire mad scientists and put them in a secluded castle in the mountains with a multi-million-dollar budget and unlimited time to tinker and experiment. That does sound fun, though.

But I would argue, and I do argue this all the time, that every company needs to set aside a small percentage of their resources for experimentation. Dedicate some energy and effort to exploring the unknown. Build a culture of innovation where it's not only OK to try offbeat ideas and it's not only expected, but it's demanded. "Let's do this because it's necessary for our evolution. And we'll see what the results are."

Unless you build that creative experimentation spirit into your company's DNA, this type of experimentation is less likely to happen. The natural tendency of corporate governance to be conservative with risk and expenditures will take over. For many of them, even if the project is a success, the juice isn't worth the squeeze. Many valuable ideas will be lost.

Companies must accept that experimentation by definition doesn't always yield hard business results. I once interviewed the head of innovation at Adidas. One of the questions I asked him was, "What are the company's expectations of your department? What are your key performance indicators (KPIs)?"

He said, "We don't have any."

Adidas has built a culture of innovation: they understand the value of innovation and experimentation for its own sake. They prize a different kind of ROI—a return on innovation. (We'll talk about Adidas's award-winning innovation, the connected soccer ball, in chapter 5.)

For innovative companies like Adidas, trust is a really important element. Top management has to trust in the process of experimentation. They need to believe in the people they hire to lead their innovation efforts. They must have faith that the team isn't wasting the company's money. In companies with a culture of experimentation and innovation, the trust is there. At least to an extent. It's like letting crazy Uncle Rick babysit your kids. Yeah, he's fun and all, but you know when you come home the house might be trashed and the kids might be up until midnight eating Hot Pockets and Gummi Worms. Despite your worries, when it's all said and done, everything turned out all right. Maybe the surprise—to your astonishment—is that the next day, little Johnny shows you the backflip he learned or his newfound love for the guitar, or he's spitting Tupac lyrics. Yes, it was messy, but now, not only do your kids have new favorite memories that will last a lifetime, they're also learning new skills that could send them to the next Olympics or street-level rap battle.

Unfortunately, not every company is comfortable taking a leap of faith into the innovation unknown. History is littered with cautionary tales of companies that played it safe and refused to take risks. In many cases, they failed to innovate because they never developed a culture of experimentation. Not every attempt at innovation will lead to a billion-dollar increase in shareholder value. But some will. And if you don't at least try, you'll never even have a chance.

Blockbuster Video had an opportunity to buy Netflix early in its life, but they took a pass. They calculated that delivering DVDs to customers would necessitate changing their whole business model and involve complicated logistics. Yes, it would. But what was the alternative? Bankruptcy, as it turns out. If Blockbuster had fostered a deep culture of experimentation, they might have jumped on the idea. When they finally got around to trying DVD delivery and streaming direct to consumers, it was too late; Netflix already owned the market.

ACQUIRE, MIMIC, OR COLLABORATE

Companies that do not foster their own innovation can still benefit from the innovations of others. There are three primary ways.

First, they can license it or acquire it. This is a strategy large tech companies like Apple and Intel utilize a lot. They buy high-tech start-ups that have developed new technologies. Or they license those technologies rather than trying to reinvent them. Google bought YouTube. Facebook bought Instagram. Twitter bought Periscope. You get the idea.

The second way companies can get innovative without doing the required radical experimentation is by mimicking. This means copying what works. In practice, companies will launch a version of something that another company is already doing, but they'll try to do it better. In 2012, a start-up called Vine launched a social platform based on short-form, looping video content. It became the go-to platform for comedy creators, fans, and brands alike. In light of Vine's success, there were a million copycats. I can't tell you the number of platforms I met with that were all about microvideos. At the same time, Instagram—which already had millions of users—took note, first launching fifteen-second video functionality, then later expanding to a full sixty seconds. Today, Vine is...well...dead on the vine.

The third way companies can get into the innovation game is by collaborating with other businesses or creators. The "eat your own brain" promotion discussed at the beginning of this chapter is a great example. Two companies joined forces to boost the awareness of both parties beyond what either one of them could have accomplished on their own.

THE TSUNAMI OF INNOVATION IS ARRIVING NOW

Every day, more individuals and companies are moving in the direction of radical experimentation. Almost every product category is experiencing innovation and advancements at a pace never seen before. Earbuds can translate languages in real time. Rollercoasters at theme parks now come with VR headsets. There are maps on your phone that tell you where to buy marijuana. Refrigerators are now smart appliances that will digitally keep track of your milk carton and automatically reorder, thanks to the internet of things. Voice-activated digital assistants are evolving into full-blown robots. At the Consumer Electronics Show in 2018, the connected vehicle space was close to 300,000 square feet, making it the largest auto show in the country. And these are just a few examples of hundreds of categories.

Part of the reason for this is our society's growing level of comfort with massive innovation and the integration of technology into our daily lives. I remember years ago when people would only pay with cash instead of credit cards because they didn't want their transactions tracked by Big Brother. Most people today are actually more comfortable typing in their credit card info to a website when they have no idea who is behind it than they are actually handing the card to another person, like a server at a restaurant. "Hey, those socks look cool! Here's my credit card, my home address, my social media profile, and (more than likely) the same password I use on every other platform."

Today, if you look at a thermos on Amazon, that thermos and twelve others just like it will follow you around the internet for weeks until you finally give up and order one. And even if you give in and buy, they still follow you around!

I was one of those people who thought text messaging was stupid when it first came out. I remember saying, "Why do I need to type in a message when I can pick up the phone and call the person?" But after trying it for a few weeks, I realized, "Wait, I don't have to talk to this person at all? It's genius!" That is an example of the holy grail of technology. It has to make life easier. It's not that people don't like change; they don't like transition.

Human beings are problem solvers. It's in our nature. We will either find problems to solve, or we'll create solutions to problems that may not necessarily exist. At least not yet. Many start-ups and tech companies are developing mind-blowing technologies, but they have yet to find an application. In my mind, that's fine. Innovation for innovation's sake is a worthy goal in and of itself. Many of those technologies will eventually find their place.

Here's an example: I once met an inventor who developed a fascinating, new, high-speed photographic technology. He was a tinkerer. He knew the technology was powerful and had potential, but he wasn't sure how to apply it to the real world. He ended up selling it to a company, which then sold it to another company that finally found a use for it. What did they use his camera technology for? A little street-level photography project. Maybe you've heard of it... It's called Google Street View in Google Maps.

Let me be clear here. Innovation is not synonymous with technology. There are numerous examples of analog culture leapfrogging itself and showing up in new ways. One of my favorite examples of this is Daybreaker dance parties, a global series of early morning, drug- and alcohol-free raves attended en masse. It's the new exercise. It's the new party. It's the new way to wake up.

As you're exploring your own science, be sure to think holistically and to mark the societal cues and curiosities that make some ideas stickier than others.

CHECKMATE OR KNOCKOUT

What would happen if you handed a pair of boxing gloves to world-famous chess champion Bobby Fischer and told him to get in the boxing ring with Mike Tyson? Well, you'd probably end up calling an ambulance. And maybe a lawyer. But you'd also have a spectacular pay-per-view event in the sport of chessboxing. Yes, chessboxing.

A central theme of this book is unlikely pairings, or oddball combinations of diverse ideas, and one of my favorites is called chessboxing. Brought to the United States from the UK, chessboxing is exactly what it sounds like. World class athletes play this combination of two very different games, so different that they were rarely even spoken of in the same conversation until this sporting event combined them. Competitors do a round of boxing, then they make a chess move, then another round of boxing. The players can win either by checkmate or knockout. It's equal parts brain and brawn.

You can watch chessboxing online. It's huge in London, often filling arenas and stadiums with tens of thousands of fans. Standing six-foot-seven, weighing in at 320 pounds, and wearing the blue trunks, the man responsible for bringing it to the United States is Andrew McGregor—more affectionately known as King Drew. He's highly ranked in the sport of boxing, and he's one of the world's top chess players. Oh, and did I tell you he's also an entrepreneur and inventor?

I interviewed King Drew on *Innovation Crush*. Drew has had a fascinating life and career. He used to run a nonprofit called the Tiziano Project, which teaches journalism to children in war-torn countries around the world. The project provides aspiring citizen journalists with cameras and equipment to tell their own stories about their communities and get them out into the world. Technology and social media have made sharing these stories to a global audience easier.

Drew spent so much time in conflict zones helping kids tell their stories that, over time, he grew numb to violence and war in the world. He saw so many awful things. Some of the kids have had their families torn apart by civil war, human trafficking, land mines, kidnapping, and political imprisonment. Some have seen relatives die in front of them. Drew told me, "I got to the point where I couldn't feel anything unless there was a gun pointed in my face."

A PUNCH TO THE GUT

In my interview with Drew, he told the story of how he woke up from his numbness. One day when he was in Los Angeles, he happened to walk past Freddie Roach's gym in Hollywood and decided to go in for a work out. While sparring, he got hit in the stomach so hard it knocked the wind out of him. Somehow, that one punch woke him up. He felt something for the first time in a long while, even if it was sharp pain.

After that, Drew devoted himself to learning boxing. After he realized he wanted to train in boxing, he wrote a cold letter to boxing great George Foreman. To his surprise, Foreman neither sent him a limited-edition, gold-plated, Alexa-enabled George Foreman grill, nor did he help Drew sign up for car insurance. (Thanks, Chris, now I've got the "1-800 General Now" jingle in my head). But the boxing legend did write Drew back and gave him a slew of tips and advice. Shortly after, Drew discovered that odd combination of two unlikely competitions called chessboxing. Today he's one of the foremost players in the world. Drew worked with the founders of chessboxing to help promote the sport, even at one point working with

RZA from the musical group Wu-Tang Clan, who happens to be an avid chess player.

Drew is a fascinating guy with a wide range of interests, ideas, and hobbies. In fact, after our chat, Drew was heading to another part of town for strongman training. You've probably seen these competitions where people flip tires and carry boulders on their backs. Or pull a rooted tree out of the ground with their bare hands or push an office building over while people are still in it. Drew invited me to come train with him.

"Sure, hold on. Just let me go get my strongman onesie and training gear out of my back seat." (Sorry, Drew. I'll get there one day.)

Through it all, Drew is a like an enthusiastic kid, and he's an incredible innovator. The bearded gentle giant wears custom-made three-piece suits. To a stranger, he might be big and intimidating. He's frightening-looking even in Savile Row pin stripes, that is, until you start talking to him. Then you discover he's a big softy. He's also ridiculously smart and has a technical mind. For example, Drew has built and deployed robots that can navigate minefields. Try that on your next free weekend.

Chess and boxing don't readily go together. That's what makes the unique combination so exciting and different.

It's like combining NASA and art. It reminds me of UCLA's Dennis Hong, who is listed by *Wired* magazine as one of the top roboticists in the world and also happens to be a magician and a bestselling author of fiction books in South Korea. Dennis puts his passions together and gives riveting lectures that combine robots, magic, and great storytelling.

These are examples of one of the central themes of this book. When you connect the dots in unusual ways, it often leads to unexpected advances and undiscovered opportunities.

"What if we took X and married it with Y?"

"Hey, how do we make money on footwear and make a difference in the world?" (Toms Shoes)

"What if we could allow every citizen to be a taxi driver?" (Uber)

Most of us aren't naturally adept at pairing these things, but innovation often explores bringing them together.

I also see a similarity between chessboxing and the innovator's path, which is equal parts "Hey, this is a smart idea" and "Oh crap, I need to really muscle this idea through in order to make it happen."

Innovation requires equal parts brains and brawn. Any idea is only as good as it is executed, which takes a lot of muscle and grit along with the emotional fortitude to stick with it. As Troy Carter once stated, "I'm looking for founders who can drive a Mack Truck through a cul-de-sac."

Drew had his goosebump moment when that punch to the gut finally made him feel something real and deep after a long period of emotional numbness. Many of us have great ideas, but not "I have to do this" ideas. Drew had no shortage of opportunities, but nothing really woke him up. He needed that gut punch. In a sense, it's what we all need.

That release of endorphins that we usually associate with love or happiness—the same thing can happen with creativity. There is a sense of elation that comes from a sudden connection with our vision, with that moment when we say, "Oh, I see something here."

In Drew's story, the physical and psychological response to getting punched impacted him profoundly, and it stuck with him. It created a new connection. It's often those things you connect with on a deep level that get you through the hard parts. Think about all of the training he had to go through as a new boxer and as a new chess player. Doing thousands of sit-ups and hours of jump rope is not the fun part. The fun part is playing the game. But the training is necessary.

For the innovator's journey, all the preparation and hard work you need to do to make that big idea happen or bring that vision to life can be a struggle. If you don't have an emotional connection to the vision, you're more likely to jump off the horse as soon as the ride gets a little rocky.

You might have an idea that doesn't connect with you deep down. As with all strong relationships, you need a strong connection to make it work. In a marriage, we say, "Till death do us part." You have plenty of ups and downs, but you're looking at this wonderful future for you and your family, and you're trying to stick to that vision because you know that there's a greater purpose and a deeper connection. Interesting ideas without that connection will probably never come to fruition.

Idea-smiths and entrepreneurs go through ups and downs; it's part of the job. Nicole Yershon, a friend of mine who is the former head of Ogilvy's Innovation Lab in the UK, has a fascinating story. She's a Cannes Gold Lions winner, a sought-after speaker, and an author whom advertising legend Dave Trott referred to as "an irresistible force against immovable objects." Nicole is one of the amazing few that have been on *Innovation Crush* twice.

Nicole is a fighter. She was battling for her budget every year just to keep her department alive, despite all the things they had done for the company and for their clients.

That ability to keep fighting for survival while still delivering world-class innovation requires a strong connection to her vision. She believed wholeheartedly in what she was doing, so the idea of quitting never even crossed her mind.

THE IDEA OF IDEAS

There came a point in time when I fell in love with the idea of ideas. I didn't care what the industry or vertical was. In fact, the more obscure, the better. Thinking about obscure concepts and oddball ideas helps flex the muscles and sharpen the creative part of the mind. Whether we needed to figure out how to build a better sleeper couch or an exciting new technology product, I always love coming up with new concepts.

My love of ideas and the innovation process includes several steps: creating the idea, then presenting that idea, and finally bringing it to life visually on a stage. I am enamored with injecting innovation into live events. I always think through how a live event could be different and better and how to make it cut through the clutter. But it all starts with the idea. I get goosebumps when I'm in a brainstorming session, and suddenly, we have a eureka moment, a brilliant idea that I know has legs.

I've had enough experiences throughout my life to empathize with virtually anyone in any room. That ability to code switch, or be a cultural chameleon, is one that's inherent in all of us. Think about how social media has allowed us all to express and discover our multihyphenate selves. Think about that friend from high school—that friend whom you've probably hated being connected to because of their weird rants and overly personal posts, but since all your other classmates are friends with him, too, you suffer from a severe case of delete guilt. Then you discover that friend works in real estate, skis, knits, somehow turned out to be a good dancer, and posts recipes. Then you write him that DM on the sly, like, "It's OK—I knit, too!"

That realization is what led me to begin my own evolution. I realized there is value in this thing that is inherently who I am, so I try not to pigeonhole myself or give my skills a specific label that I think others will readily identify with. There is much more to all of us than what's listed on our résumés or what former colleagues might recognize us for.

Because I've experienced so many different walks of life, had so many unusual jobs, and experienced so many different life circumstances, I am able to connect dots where others see no connection at all. I've been a meandering observer, so I'm primed to make these connections. I first practiced this skill while doing stand-up comedy. I took me a while to realize this is an invaluable skill in the business world.

A journalist for the website Breakout once interviewed me and asked about responsible idea development. I told him, "Your responsibility is to put as much of yourself into your ideas as possible. Understand who you are and what your perspectives are." Just like with chess and boxing, I believe all sides of a person can be combined and contained in the development of an idea.

For example, if you're a chef, you're not just an expert at cooking; you're also an expert at putting different ingredients together. The more unique the combo, the more surprisingly delicious the experience. Or if you are a teacher-cum-entrepreneur, maybe you're amazingly adept at breaking down complex concepts into palatable chunks—a skill that is valuable when talking to folks like investors, collaborators, or the press.

INNOVATION IS NO JOKE

I attended a leadership training event one weekend, and one of the participants in the training program was an Olympic decathlete. He mentioned that he's a personal trainer and trains people in boxing. (Not chessboxing—that would be an extremely weird coincidence.) At first, that struck me as odd because there's no boxing in the decathlon. Upon further thought, it makes sense because no matter what kind of athlete you are, you train other muscles even if the exercises might not always be related to your primary sport. Just like a decathlete might cross-train by boxing or swimming, you must train a wide range of muscles that you don't use regularly to excel at creativity.

As a swimmer myself, I do a lot of workouts on land. I'm on a master swim team, and many of my teammates do all sorts of bike rides, running, or yoga, plus sit-ups and push-ups and other strength exercises before we get into the water. It makes sense because we put ourselves into a different environment and work different muscles than when we're swimming, which makes us stronger all around.

Creativity works the same way. Give yourself more experiences so you can understand more things and ultimately connect more dots.

Try this: as an exercise, pick two random objects and try to list as many similarities in them as possible. Make a bullet-point list with ten blank lines and write one similarity in each until every blank is filled.

For example, a cell phone and a car. They both have wires. They both have plastic in them. They both require batteries. They both have screens. You get the idea. Keep going until your list pushes the boundaries of your creativity. This exercise starts to help you develop your creativity muscles. If you do bicep curls every week, your biceps are going to get stronger. It's the same with creativity.

Feel free to try this exercise on your own. A Frisbee and clock. A squirrel and a basketball. Make yourself a basket of words and pull out a random pair and begin the exercise. It's a creative brain workout you can do with your team to jump-start any brainstorming session.

That's why I've ventured into territories often unfamiliar to me in my career, constantly stretching past my comfort zone to learn new things. If you work at an art museum, go to a Bitcoin conference. If you're an English teacher, go to the hot rod show in Las Vegas. Get as many different life perspectives as you can; they will pay dividends later. You never know, maybe museums will start accepting cryptocurrency, or you can create a board of education hot rod league.

I have a tattoo that reads, "Change the way you look at things, and the things you look at will begin to change." That concept is core to my life philosophy, and it's been a big boost to my career. The best way to change the way you look at things is to deliberately go out and seek new experiences—especially unfamiliar experiences. As you do, you will automatically begin the process of seeing the world around you differently. That is one of the most important steps the in the innovator's journey. You'll be surprised at the new ideas that begin to pop up when you stretch yourself.

BECOME A MERCENARY

Question: What do you get when you combine Fat Albert and Albert Einstein? Answer: you get Hakeem Oluseyi. He was poor, tall, lanky, and nerdy, growing up in areas where it's not safe to go outside if you want to avoid getting in trouble. Throughout his childhood, he moved several times to such luxurious hoods ranging from Watts, New Orleans's ninth ward; South Central; Houston; and a few others in between.

Out of necessity, Hakeem trained his imagination to take him someplace else. It was a way to escape from the places he grew up. He moved around a number of times, so he was often the new kid in a bad neighborhood, which made it even more dangerous. Instead of going outside, Hakeem played it safe, mostly staying indoors watching television. He gravitated toward shows about Albert Einstein and series that explained how the universe works. But he also liked Fat Albert. And he loved hip-hop.

Something about science really resonated with Hakeem. He was basically a closeted supernerd, graduating as valedictorian from his high school. He went on to earn undergraduate degrees in mathematics and physics from Tougaloo College in Mississippi. Then on to Stanford, where he was the only Black kid in his master's degree program. He was also the only one in the program who didn't come from a long lineage of family physicists or legacies from colleges that didn't rhyme with boogaloo.

He always felt out of place, even in college. At one point, he wanted to drop out of Stanford. He once told the story of when he was sitting in front of the professor's office waiting for the professor to show up so he could tell him he was dropping out. Another professor passed by at that moment and struck up a conversation.

"Hey, what's going on? Are you all right?"

"Yeah," Hakeem replied. "I'm thinking about dropping out."

That professor ended up talking to him and convinced him to stay. Now Hakeem is one of the most renowned astrophysicists in the world, manages NASA's science education program, hosts television's *Outrageous Acts of Science*, and served a number of years as the chief science officer for the Discovery Channel. He's had an incredible career, leading some of the world's most important science exploration and translating geek speak into cool tools and vice versa.

Hakeem refers to himself as an industry mercenary because he has so many different skills that he's learned to bring to the table, depending on what the situation calls for. For much of his life, Hakeem was kind of like a misfit toy that didn't belong anywhere, and then not only did he find a home, he damn near built one from scratch.

Like most PhDs, Hakeem has spent a lot of time explaining things to up-and-coming science mavens. He wasn't a teacher by trade, but when he did guest lectures, he realized that the auditoriums were always packed. He wondered why that was. He realized that he has a talent for connecting students with science. Now he teaches all over the world and even visits prisons to teach science to inmates. During our *Innovation Crush* interview—which was a blast by the way—I asked him why his teaching resonates so well with people.

"I don't talk like a scientist. I talk like the people where I'm from."

Oftentimes when somebody gives you a dose of their

mind-bending knowledge, you feel blown away and probably a little stupider than before you encountered them. I told him that all of his lectures and talks that I've listened to actually made me feel smarter. He's one of those rare people who can elevate your thinking just by being in his gravitational vicinity. It never feels like he's smarter than you even though his brain could beat your brain up any day. It's a tremendous skill to meet people where they are and have them feel like they're a peer of yours. It's a trait that's both endearing and empowering.

SKILLS THAT THRILL

For about a year, I recorded my show inside the Improv Comedy Club on Melrose Avenue in Los Angeles. That's where my studio was located. After I finished interviewing Hakeem, he asked me about the venue and why we recorded there. I explained that Levity Entertainment Group owns roughly 30 percent of the comedy clubs in the country, and Levity also happens to be the parent company of the studio that produces my podcast. Levity had a network called the Sideshow Network where they housed all of their podcasts. Most of the content was comedy talent, but I was their first experiment in a new content direction. They had wanted to do something with business or politics, and they decided I would be a great fit.

Super unexpected, he then told me how he was interested

in doing stand-up comedy. He said he'd been thinking about it for a while. In addition to his numerous abilities, Hakeem also has a sharp sense of humor. I told him I thought it was a great idea and made as many introductions as I could right then and there. Hakeem is already a TV personality, life coach, writer, keynote speaker, and voice actor. So why not a comedian, too?

Hakeem has all of these different abilities and talents. He can go into a prison and speak to hardened inmates or go into a school and talk to kids just as confidently as he can stroll into a boardroom. People will have the same level of response in any environment. That's why he calls himself a science and innovation mercenary—he can be called into action anywhere at any time and accomplish the mission, pulling out whatever tools he needs to get the job done. Jokes. Hard science. Teaching skills. Rap battles. You name it.

Hakeem has another trait I really admire. He is playful, energetic, brilliant, and almost spastic. It's almost like he's *Flubber* in real life. Too often, people forget to be playful in the business world.

During that same leadership training I mentioned earlier, the facilitator said, "When you were a baby, you were nothing but joy, and then life happened."

For many of us, that couldn't be truer. Suddenly, you're

holding down a job you're not passionate about, answering to people you never imagined you would in a home you never imagined yourself in, reliving past hurts, and getting fatter than you ever thought you'd be. With all this life happening, we forget to keep being playful.

Children get in trouble sometimes, they fall down and get hurt, but they go right back outside and keep playing. They're quick to forgive and move past temporary setbacks. As adults, we run the risk of losing that spirit of adventure and play. I admire people like Hakeem who have never lost that childlike wonder and playful spirit.

I had a chance to interview Apple cofounder Steve Wozniak at the C2 Montreal conference in Canada. Before we sat down to talk, I watched him interacting with people. With each conversation, he had an awe and wonder that was like he just discovered humans' ability to speak.

The very first thing I said to him was, "You know what I like about you? You're like a big kid."

And sure enough, he went into a three-minute-long riff on why playfulness is such an important part of his life.

Every mercenary faces challenges and obstacles that can divert him or her from the core mission. When life is staring us in the face, it's easy to leave our free-spiritedness at the door and forget all the wonderful tools we have at our disposal. However, the practice of continually finding new ways to restore and express our playful spirit can enhance our lives and our careers.

KNOW ENOUGH TO BE DANGEROUS

You don't need to be an expert in everything. Just know enough to be dangerous. If that sounds negative, let me explain what I mean.

I had a mentor who was working during the height of the music video industry—this was when Notorious B.I.G. could afford a fish tank filled with mermaids swimming around in the background of his videos. My mentor was one of the foremost video producers, and as such, his job was to bring all the different resources together for the project, managing budgets, timelines, creative, talent, industry relations, and production staff.

To do this required a broad range of knowledge. He could talk to a lighting technician about what kind of lighting package was necessary for a certain mood or look. Even though he was not technically a lighting expert and didn't know lighting as well as the specialist did, he knew enough to have that conversation. He could have intelligent conversations with grips, camera operators, the special effects and pyrotechnics team, even hair and makeup. He knew enough about all of these different areas of specialized information because he had to. He developed a wide range of expertise, and that was a strength that made him very successful.

When it came to this kind of managerial and organizational skillset, he knew just enough to have intelligent conversations, while remaining naïve enough not to be limited by the way things are usually done. He was continually hacking methods to get things done faster, cheaper, or altogether differently. Therein lay a duality that stretched the creativity of everyone involved.

He would ask things like, "Why can't we use this lighting package instead of that one?"

The lighting people would respond, "Hmmm...you know what? We've never thought about doing it that way because we've always done it this way."

Then they would get to contributing ideas for ways to accomplish whatever the producer needs, perhaps even creating a whole new way to light a scene. That's the power of knowing enough about how something works while also being naïve enough to think about it from a totally different perspective.

That wide range of knowledge also protects you from

losing your shirt on an idea or project. Any lean start-up founder or even semi-dumb podcast host will tell you this. I was developing a virtual reality project a while back, so I called a production company that came highly recommended.

I told them the budget we had, and almost immediately, they replied, "That's not enough. It can't be done like that. You need a minimum of at least double that budget."

I knew enough to realize there was a way to get it done on that budget. Of course, I didn't know exactly how. I called a friend at a different company, Two Bit Circus. I filled him in on my quagmire, and together, we reengineered both the creative and the technology in the project, figured out what to trim, and made it work under that budget, affirming what I initially believed. I asked every dumb question I could think of and offered up every creative cheat that came to mind. Each met with equal amounts of expertise and wonder. Not only did we manage to save that project, they've become one of my favorite collaborators for numerous projects over the years.

INNOVATION MEETS LIMITATION

I am lucky to work with many individuals and companies who are willing to try new things and consider novel ideas.

That's what innovation is all about, and sometimes it comes from strict limitations.

A reporter interviewed me for an article in *Forbes* magazine about innovation. I said that some of the best innovation comes from constraint. In other words, when you don't have enough time, you don't have enough money, or you don't have enough resources, but you still need to figure it out. In those situations, you should become well versed in many things because you may not be able to have a dedicated specialist in each part of a project. You may need to cheat a little, or at least use a completely different method in order to get the same results for less time and money.

In an advisory capacity, knowing just enough has opened up countless opportunities for me. I can advise companies, design eCommerce platforms, or even help think of a better way to build household appliances. If you know just enough about a wide range of subjects, you can innovate in whatever's within your proximity.

For example, during the Global Entrepreneurship Summit, I sat with a company from Haiti that redesigned the standard kitchen oven specifically for the Haitian market. As a resident of Haiti, the company founder had the advantage of proximity, so she was able to design a product perfectly suited to the uniqueness of that country.

AN EXPLORER, NOT AN EXPERT

Sometimes, asking dumb questions leads to break-throughs. You can't innovate in a vacuum. You can't tinker away at your idea, then open the garage and announce, "Look, here it is." Open yourself up to criticism. Some of the best advice you can get comes from people asking dumb questions. Be willing to hear all of the things you're probably afraid to hear.

Sometimes we hold back for fear of having an idea stolen, fear of embarrassment, or fear of failure. I once wrote a spec script for *That '70s Show*, which I personally thought was pretty darned good. I knew there was a chance the ideas in the script could be ripped off, but I shared it anyway. I sent it to would-be agents. I let friends read it. I even tried to explain to my mom what a spec script was. Eventually I had a chance to share it with the studio that produced the show—the holy grail of submitting your spec script.

A few months later, while I was in Detroit for the holiday, some friends came over to my parents' home. While we were hanging out and catching up, the TV was on, my back facing the screen.

Suddenly, one friend said, "Hey...wasn't that in your script?"

I turned around toward the TV, and for the next twenty

minutes, we watched a good majority of the episode I wrote play out on television. No check. No phone call. No email.

Ironically, something in me was elated. Despite the utter shock and disappointment, it was extremely flattering to know that I was talented enough to be stolen from! Even though I had experienced the downside of exploration and putting myself out there, I got some pretty good feedback in sort of a messed-up way. At the same time, like many of us should, I believe in creative abundance and the notion that many of my best ideas are ahead of me. To exchange one of them for a bit of affirmation was like that sixth night we talked about in the beginning. I had been bombing up until then, but now I was back!

DON'T BREAK THE RULES—SHATTER THEM

"I don't fake it till I make it, I take it to the limit and break it."
—BLACK THOUGHT, THE ROOTS

My career has taken me to places that, on paper, I have no business being. In no particular order, I've had a marketing agency and a DJ business. I've advised the White House, produced music, mentored Google's Launchpad, sold real estate, consulted political systems, won awards for virtual reality, partnered with Intel to design artwork, managed talent, helped Walmart showcase the future of retail, and even traveled to Buenos Aires to give a forty-five-minute talk (which I woke up late for, but still nailed). Let's not forget that for a number of years, this all felt like a near-depression state of meandering and doing whatever I could to survive.

For many people, my professional journey breaks the rules of conventional career paths. When it comes to helping others break rules, my oddball collection of experiences helps me bring a broad swath of insights I've picked up along the way. When I'm working with founders of start-ups or, let's say, artificial intelligence pioneers, the risk is that I may not know exactly how the technology or product works that I'm talking about. But that's not required. You become your own science experiment.

Say, "I'm going to do the best I can. I believe wholeheartedly in the value of my experience thus far, and I'm not afraid to look foolish."

Fear of perception can be a heavy beast on the back of any innovator. Letting go of it can be one of the most freeing moves you'll ever make.

You ever felt like you totally blew a presentation or a pitch or a date with a would-be lover, and the next day, those very people told you how amazingly well you did? Maybe you took a test in school that you undoubtedly knew you failed, and then you got an A? There have been times when I'm in my car, rushing to the studio, frantically researching the topic and the guest at red lights along the route. I consider myself a professional, but at the same time, I don't want to appear unprepared. I don't want to miss that one nugget I should have had ready to bring up as a topic of conversation, or I just want to simply pronounce their name right.

Many times, these are the interviews where my mind is like, "WTF are you doing, Chris?" But then, a few minutes in, something greater takes over. Surprisingly, some of those interviews turn out to be among my best. Maybe it's the hours of putting core skills into practice, maybe it's muscle memory, maybe it's subconscious connection or luck, or maybe it's all of those things. The point is, the rules and limitations we put on ourselves are only mirages, and the more we push ourselves outside our comfort level, the more strength we gather to break the rules.

Like any mercenary, sometimes you survive and thrive on sheer nerves and grit alone.

REAL-WORLD *CADDYSHACK*

No disrespect to the fine folks at the Southfield Eccentric who fired me for throwing away the newspapers instead of delivering them, but my very first real job was caddying at Oakland Hills Country Club. Oakland Hills to this day is the number one country club in Michigan and home of the 1996 US Open. Working there was one of the biggest juxtapositions in my life.

Like most metropolises, Detroit is made up of many parts: there's an inner city, surrounded by suburbs, inspiring cultural corners, fancy waterfront properties, and one of the largest multicultural populations I've seen in the country. In fact, I went to high school with white kids, Blacks, Jews, Chaldeans, and everything in between. I even had an Armenian French teacher—figure that one out. *Bonjour Madame Sesi!*

Thus, many of the caddies I worked with at Oakland Hills came from all over the area, from Detroit and from the suburbs. Some of them were kids who were well off; others were guys who had recently gotten out of jail. We had a seventy-year-old man known simply as "Foots." And that was the life. We all had nicknames, and we all got along.

As a caddie, you're often spending anywhere from two to ten hours a day walking around and talking with some of the most successful people in the state, if not the world. From local heroes like Detroit Piston legend Bill Laimbeer to celebrities like Leslie Nielsen and Michael Jordan, or families who are rich AF from making corrugated boxes or the fabric that goes on the visor in your car. #truefacts

The clubhouse was Elysium. All the socialites, aristocrats, and fabric mavens snorting up all the good oxygen and dining on the skins of newborn babies (a delicacy I hear about in some circles). In contrast, the caddie shack actually has the word "shack" in it, so I'm sure you get the picture. A place to get hot dogs or soda, play pinball, cash in your chits, and wait till you're called up for another loop. In "da shack," (We didn't actually call it that, but allow me to embellish a bit here. It's my book!), we'd be playing video games and cards, gambling, or expressing hilarious forbidden intentions with each other's moms. Then we'd straighten up our collars and go to work with very successful people.

The ability to leave a game of Tunk and go advise a corporate CEO on how to win $10,000 in a golf tournament taught me a great deal about how to deal with diverse groups of people. Listening as a skill. Awareness of your audience and environment. How to speak to people in their own languages. And through it all, still be yourself. I think we all have that potential to get outside our perceived comfort zones and thrive in any environment we're thrust into.

I started caddying when I was thirteen and probably did my last round shortly after I graduated college. Caddying paid for my first car. It got me onto the golf team at my high school. (Go Chargers!) It got me engineering interviews.

It got me tickets to the US Open! Plus, early on, that ten-mile bike ride six days a week to work a ten-hour day had my hamstrings on fleek.

As much as I love Detroit, as with any city, it had its downsides. When I was in elementary school, I remember pulling into the driveway (no I wasn't driving) and seeing my next-door neighbor attempting to break into our house. In high school, I was robbed at gunpoint behind my school. I've been at parties where people decided to start shooting. I was even in a high-speed car chase. I was basically the Jason Bourne of the 313, although ironically, I've actually never been in fight!

At the same time, Detroit is synonymous with some amazing things: the pioneering auto industry, the birth of some of my favorite brands like Shinola and Rock Ventures, and of course, it's the city that gave us Motown. Not only that, Detroit gave rise to house music and EDM, and did you know that the first mall in the world was opened in Detroit? Boom! Now that's what I call a "hot topic." Today, Detroit has companies like LinkedIn and Microsoft setting up shop, and even rising industries like robotics and accelerators are calling the city home.

Therein lies another great duality. We take the good and the bad, and we turn them both into our strengths. We allow our life experiences to inform our overall perspective. How can I be upset about an idea not going the way I planned when I've almost died? Not that I'm focused on those memories per se or even look upon them negatively, but the resiliency I've been blessed to develop plays a huge part in how I operate as an individual, in life and business.

On *Innovation Crush*, this topic comes up often. Both sides of the coin of life are constantly in motion, and the hardships we've survived subconsciously inform how we express our creativity. I've heard stories of depression, cancer survival, fractured spines, car accidents, molestation, parental suicides, disabilities, divorce, and everything in between from some of the people I admire most in the world when it comes to innovation. In every interview, there's a surprise plot twist in our conversation where a skill from someone's past hardship shows up later in their life to contribute to their success.

No matter what you've been through, no matter how rough you've had it, no matter where you are today, don't look back on those experiences as all negative. Rather, think about the good that came out of them. Did they make you stronger? Did they show you that you could survive anything and keep moving forward? There is almost always a positive that comes out of every negative life experience.

KICK SOME BALLS

Now more than ever, companies all over the world are venturing into innovation, which is a wonderful thing. But when they do, they often hinder their own efforts by immediately trying to apply standard business restrictions and measurements. They want to assess the results, create a set of business goals, such as, "What's our ROI? When will this task be completed?" The business world is full of limitations, from finite budgets to deadlines to a minimum expected return on every dollar spent.

Investors want numbers, bosses want deliverables, and every founder's family wants to eat. It's understandable; how else will we know if our innovation efforts are working? The truth is, we won't. At least not always, and maybe that's a good thing. Forcing creativity and innovation to meet the same outcomes as more measurable practices like sales is like throwing a wet blanket on the creative process. It hinders ideas.

It's the age-old question: What would you create if you had no limits?

NO PRESSURE

When I asked Jon Werner about this, his answer just about made me jealous. Jon's official title is innovation explorer for global shoe and sportswear giant Adidas.

I said to him, "Your job is to innovate at a big company that's globally renowned for sportswear, so what sort of expectations or KPIs does the company hold you to? You're not simply experimenting for the sake of experimenting, right?"

He smirked. "We don't have any expectations."

He was the first to give this answer. But he would not be the last.

Jon has the ability to go out and be as wildly creative as his heart desires, as long as it's practical for the company. He has no deadlines, no performance standards, no ROI demands. And that structure has led to some great projects. One of the most prized innovations his department came up with was a connected soccer ball, and it was a CES Innovation Award winner.

The connected soccer ball uses sensors to measure each kick's impact, speed, and rotation, as well as recording the wind, temperature, and other metrics that are key to athletic performance. The ball even offers corrections: "Next time try hitting the ball with your instep instead of your toe." This wildly successful product is now used by soccer coaches and players worldwide.

There's something to be said for letting the people you work with do what they do best and not worrying about whether projects are going to be delivered in disastrous fashion. You've probably heard the term "helicopter parent" used to describe parents who smother their children by constantly hovering over them. If you've ever stood over a creative director's shoulder while he or she worked on your logo, guess what? You're now a helicopter parent. Or maybe a helicopter manager. I can definitely say I've been guilty as charged. This is different than micromanagement and having your grubby little hands in every step along the way. Helicopter managers are just there, lurking, checking in, and waiting for the slightest reason to pull the plug. Along the way, any spark of innovation starts to diminish due to this silent pressure of having someone watching everything they do. Sometimes we're our own helicopter manager, questioning every decision we've made or intend to make.

Of course, there's no such thing as blind faith in business ecosystems. There shouldn't be. At the same time, letting the innovation team work in their own way means you have to (a) hire the right people who can be fiscally responsible and (b) know that investing in the wrong people or innovation ecosystem will kill your investment. You need a mix of the right individuals plus creative freedom, plus trust and accountability. I understand that some of this might be counterintuitive. Of course we want to run our businesses efficiently and get a return on every dollar spent. I get that. But there's also another form of ROI: Return on Innovation, which we'll get into later in the chapter.

Here's an example. My college roommate, whom I've known for twenty years and was best man in my wedding, recently got married. I hadn't prepared a speech, and I hadn't done stand-up or even nonbusiness public speaking in a very long time. Even after having pondered for days and knowing this guy for half my life, I didn't know what to say or how the speech would go. I wrote some things on a piece of paper that I planned to read in front of the crowd because I really wanted to create a memorable moment.

At the reception, I got up in front of the crowd and talked

through the first couple of bullet points on the paper. But then, like every triumphant movie from the 1990s, I decided to throw the paper away and speak from the heart instead.

Cue triumphant music and slow zoom in.

I ignored the expectations and the need to perform. Yes, I wanted him and his bride to feel warm and entertained by my words. I wanted to create that "aww" moment. But I also realized I could just be me. Plus, the open bar helped. Soon after, I heard that first chuckle, and next thing you know, I was having a blast. We like to razz each other, so I made fun of him, I made fun of her. It was no holds barred, both in terms of tenderness and insult. I think it was a fair mix of the two. At least I hope. (Guys, do you forgive me?)

I believe the speech went better than expected because I made a conscious decision to put myself in a relaxed space where I put very little expectation on myself, and nobody else put any expectation on me. That relaxed state is where creatives do their best work—not when the ghetto bird is buzzing overhead.

FREEDOM TO CREATE

This same principle applies to the business world. Sometimes boosting innovation requires structuring your company in a way that makes people feel free to create. It also involves running a team where the brainstorm space is the safest space; nobody gets upset when someone brings up a random topic or unrelated idea. At my brainstorm sessions, for example, you'll never hear, "Oh, I hate it when Joe starts talking about chocolate chips in our meetings." Let Joe talk about chocolate chips! It might end up being the nugget of a billion-dollar idea someday.

There should be these kinds of creative safe spaces within your business—spaces where there's no worry about outcome, even if you're up against tight, real-world deadlines. I've been in situations where some walks into my office like Lumbergh from the movie *Office Space*. "Umm, yaaah. I know today is Monday. I'm gonna need ideas by the end of day Tuesday because we're going to meet the client first thing Wednesday morning. Thanks." I can't tell you the number of times I've gone back to revisit an idea and thought, "I wish I had more time."

As intense of a situation as that can be, you still allow yourself the emotional space to not internalize that kind of pressure. Deadlines like that are a fact of life in many businesses; the key is to prevent them from putting a damper on the creative process. There will always be occasions when you wish you had more time or where you think of a better idea two weeks later, but if you allow yourself to be free from the burden of expectation, then you establish a creative zone.

The key is to create the feeling of freedom despite high-stress circumstances. Once you enter that brainstorm space, let go of the expectation for a minute—literally block it out of your mind. Lifting that burden from yourself and your team allows you to still be creatively expressive without the pressure. That worry, if you let it, will kill the creativity.

That ability to block out external stressors is another muscle that you can strengthen. Once you go through enough high-stress situations, you learn how to deal with them. You get better at it. Professional golfers are a good example of learning to deal with intense scrutiny. Imagine if you had to do your very best work while five hundred people were standing twenty feet away, watching your every move. They learn to block out the pressure and not let it bother them. But developing that skill takes time and practice.

I've had a number of instances when I had to get things done at the last minute because something was suddenly due the next day. I either stayed up late or got up early and got into the zone. Allow yourself to get into the creative zone, uninhibited by deadline stress, even if it's only for an hour or two. Maybe the presentation won't be fully formulated, but at least you'll have some bullet points to explain the basics of the idea. Practice allowing yourself to get in a flow despite external circumstances.

I started doing yoga a short while ago, and learning to quiet the noise (internal or external) to get into a flow is a big part of yoga practice. The instructors will say things like, "This pose hurts, and yes, it's hard, but keep breathing." The next thing you know, you're balancing on a pinky toe with one arm behind your head and a big smile on your face. There are even smaller cues that almost go unnoticed. The first time I was told to relax my forehead, or my tongue, I was like, "Relax my tongue? Who tenses their—oh, I do." The whole idea here is to have some self-awareness about the types of things we don't even realize are adding to our overall stress or discomfort in any moment.

On the other hand, there's something to be said about a good emotional and mental challenge—like being pushed to your limit and proving you can still deliver. It's the world Andy Walshe plays in. That competitive edge is something we all have within us to deliver our best selves and win no matter what.

I always have this vision in the back of my mind in which the person receiving the idea tells me how awesome it is, and I reply, "Yes, and we didn't have a lot of time to get it done." In my mind, it's a little bit of an "I told you so" moment. Not only that, I'm excited about the process because I know that, despite the time crunch and limitations, the end result will be awesome and well received even though I know we could probably do more with more time. "You want to give me difficult conditions? Okay, watch what I do now." Focusing on positive outcomes and happy clients is one way to block out the stress of having to create on a deadline.

Note to anyone I work with who might be reading this: don't get it twisted. I will push back if you make a ridiculously tight request.

THUNDER THURSDAYS

When I was at Machinima, I created something that I find very helpful to the creative process. It was a two-hour, weekly session I called "Thunder Thursdays." My team would go to a different spot in the building or outside or even to some offsite location, and we'd have our brainstorm sessions there. The idea is to get out of our usual space. This physical change of location helps signal a clean break—even if only temporary—from the norms of the office.

I've even heard of creative teams having walking meetings. Hmmm. I'm not so sure about that one. I just have this image in my mind of a pack of early morning Golden Girls in LA Gear track suits swishing through a mall before it opens. Except instead of talking about Blanche's date, they're having a conversation about spreadsheets and conference calls. But then again, the point is to get outside your comfort zone, so...maybe I'm the weirdo.

On Thunder Thursdays, we had no agenda. We could come up with ideas about anything. Funny what people come up with when you take the restraints off. Personal interests. Weirdo tendencies. Business ideas. Nonprofits they wanted to start. Song ideas. All kinds of mad goodness. As a result, I learned a lot about my coworkers and developed even closer relationships. Plus, by hearing each other out and talking through each person's thoughts, we all got a chance to flex a different set of creative muscles.

In contrast, I've been in rooms that don't have an effective brainstorming process because the team has been meeting the same way for so long that it's become routine. Routine can be the enemy of creativity. Doing the same drills in the same conference room with the same people and with the exact same parameters doesn't exactly foster creativity. It's always the same: step one, step two, step three. Nobody can reimagine effectively that way. Taking my teams to different locations for ideation sessions has been effective and is worth the time, effort, and even resources, if need be.

THERE ARE NO BAD IDEAS

In one particular Thunder Thursday session, I had an idea that I called "the Toe Truck." At a time when food trucks were really taking off, my idea was to have a mobile manicure and pedicure salon. (I told you I was big on puns.) I shared it with the group. It was totally off topic from anything we were working on, but that was the point. For the sake of the exercise, my team went to work.

Someone challenged, "What do you do with the used water?"

Someone else said, "It will be sustainable, and it will be water-free. Or maybe we'll use mist."

We kept riffing and developing the idea. Never mind that this conversation was taking place inside of a fanboy entertainment company; we were talking about manicures and pedicures! It was an exercise in the free-spirited exploration of new ideas. A little later in the same session, after we got our creativity flowing, while talking about the Toe Truck, the conversation changed to how it could be a cool meeting place. Then we began to discuss how a lot of people in the company don't know who all the other employees are. At the time, the company was growing by leaps and bounds.

"What if we had a space dedicated to gaming and internal

meet-and-greets? You get randomly paired with another employee you don't know, then the two of you go play *Call of Duty* for thirty minutes."

Even with a free flow of ideas, we would always somehow meander back to something that was beneficial for the company.

In most of ideation sessions, one of two things happens: either we hit a magic idea at the very beginning and keep going for the sake of being thorough, or we look at the white board at the end of the meeting and think, "Well, that was a waste of ninety minutes."

Almost every idea seems like garbage, except maybe bits and pieces of two or three. However, having the freedom to put garbage on the white board is essential. You can take a couple pieces of that garbage, connect the dots between them, and discover something that works. In too many meetings I've seen, those half-baked thoughts don't even make it onto the paper or the white board. From now on, if you're the scribe, write that garbage down! If you're not the scribe, tell the scribe to write that garbage down!

Basically, don't be afraid of a thought that isn't a magic bullet or doesn't appear to immediately solve the problem. That free-thought process just might lead you to the thing that will solve the problem. If you automatically go, "No, that idea won't work," then you've lost the creative flow and hindered the free expression of the group.

Don't be totally married to your ideas or to the process by which you arrive at your ideas. "I only brainstorm on Thursdays after lunch when I'm wearing my pink socks with the unicorn on the big toe." On the other hand, you should also be aware of when and where you and your team are the most creative so you can schedule brainstorm sessions at your peak and in the right environment. Is it first thing in the morning or after a catered lunch in the conference room? But please—no more Friday at 4:00 p.m. meetings, either. Groaner!

FREE IDEA ALERT!

There's a game I've always wanted to play that I think will amp up the creativity in brainstorming sessions. You take an old TV show and say, "Hey, what if *Happy Days* were to come out in 2018? What would you do? How would you market that show? How would it exist as a brand and not just a TV series?" Remember how Arthur 'The Fonz' Fonzarelli would hit the jukebox instead of putting money in it and it would come to life? Maybe the 2018 show would have a bump function on Spotify, so if you bop your phone, it goes to the next song. No need to hit the fast-forward button. You could take advantage of the popularity of food trucks, so maybe Pat Morita has a Japanese-American fusion food truck that goes around town, or there's an Arnold's diner on wheels. Maybe you could build Tinder profiles for Joanie and Chachi. We could change the voice of Siri to the voice of Mr. Cunningham, the wise old dad: "Hey, Richie, you got a problem?" Now, Mr. Cunningham is assisting you in your life.

The idea behind this exercise is to explore how you can take advantage of culture to expand an idea. How could it exist on other platforms and experiences? It's a worthwhile exercise for stretching your creativity. Having different people in the room participate in the exercise will produce ideas that you never would have thought of. It's fun to think outside the usual thought patterns and draw on diverse perspectives to expand an idea far beyond where it started.

Many companies I encounter are focused only on their core product or domain. One start-up I met with recently designed a camera that could photograph in an art venue, so you could take a virtual tour on a tablet or your desktop.

I posed a question, "Could you do this at festivals or malls? Theme parks? Fitness facilities? What about at a Westfield shopping center? They have shopping malls around the world and retailers are dying to get people back into the brick-and-mortar spaces."

Immediately, you could see a switch go on in their heads.

They're so close to the art community that they hadn't really considered a broader application of the product, which was birthed in the art world and built within the art world...by artists. Even their marketing lead comes from within the art world. Venturing outside their domain to drum up new markets had never occurred to them. I was thinking outside of the normal confines they were used to. In many cases like this, expanding our vision not only changes the way we think about our product or service—it changes how we approach problem solving altogether.

NO WORK-LIFE BALANCE

There is tremendous value in open exploration. And although the thought of that might seem easier said than done, it can fairly easily become a bit of our everyday lives. Jon Werner does something with his team that he calls "Trend Treks." He takes his team on field trips to different locations where they observe different businesses. For instance, they might walk down Rodeo Drive going in and out of stores, observing and looking around at everything. What is the ambience? What is the floor made out of? Who's in the store? What are the people who work there wearing? How are the products displayed? Are there any interesting uses of technology? Or lighting? What does it smell like? What are other customers doing? What kind of music is playing? After each Trek, Jon facilitates a conversation around all these different characteristics.

While it's part of his job to do this on a regular basis, for the remainder of us, the idea is to become a thoughtful observer. We do it all the time anyway. Think of all the times you've complained to a family member or friend about some bad experience in a store. Think of the times that you came home excited about a really unique display, some artwork you saw, or that picture you took of something amazing that you posted on Instagram. We're constantly paying attention to how things make us feel anyway, so we may as well put it to use. It won't necessarily result in any sort of immediate relevance to an assignment or project, but there's still value in it.

At the same time, you always have the option to be more deliberate. Go stand in that line at the ninety-nine-cent store, go see how tattoo parlors operate, or go see how customers are treated at an amusement park. Visit the Grove in Los Angeles with new eyes, or Eataly in New York, Boston, Chicago, or Los Angeles. What ideas and best practices can you take from those experiences and implement into whatever project you're working on? And if you really want to step it up, call and set up a tour for yourself.

There's a quote from Nicole Yershon that I use to promote her podcast episode: "There's no work-life balance. It's all just life." Nicole explained that people go through all kinds of ups and downs in life, from giving birth to taking family with you on a business trip to being diagnosed with an illness while also working and building a career. I'd also like to think of this in the sense that the mundane things we do on a daily basis are valuable inputs to the things we experience in business. Life and work life are often intertwined, and they're both essential parts of life.

Taking this idea another layer deep, everything we go through in work and in life becomes a teachable moment that we can learn from to become better all-around human beings. All of the things we do at work—our time, our ability to be creative and innovative—echoes in other things we do in our lives.

You might go home in a great creative flow, then suddenly your wife shares a problem from her day, and soon you have a solution ready to go because you've been in the spirit of creating. Everything you observe can inform another moment or project that you're thinking about. That's one of the reasons Jon's Trend Treks idea is so productive and valuable.

TRUST ISSUES

Sometimes KPIs run the risk of simply becoming a way to keep employees in check, a way to say, "You'd better do this, this, and this by this time, or else your time and your effort is not valuable."

Maybe that's a bit extreme, but it often feels this way to

those of us on the receiving end. Or sometimes it's the boss or an investor insisting that things are done by his rules and exactly the way he wants them done. This book is all about breaking those kinds of rules. Sadly, many companies can't see the value in giving creative (and often times noncreative) employees a wide latitude to innovate. That's why trust is such a huge piece of this.

To make matters worse, if you're charged with venturing into or building the unknown, there's no way to fully anticipate the hiccups or wins you'll experience along the way. I mean, Christopher Columbus set sail on a crapshoot of a mission, and look what happened. Understandably, it's hard to have trust in a seemingly freewheeling, exploratory process of innovation. Clients or investors have their own perceptions of how the process should work. They want certain parameters in place to make sure we deliver. Meanwhile, it can be hard to have it all make sense until some sort of result is delivered.

As inventors, we can counterbalance these trust issues with more proactive information. There's a balance between needing to give stakeholders enough information to make them feel comfortable while ensuring them that we have their best interests at heart and needing to be left alone for a little while to create freely. Trust goes both ways. Each client and each creative team will find the right balance that works for them and their team.

Sometimes companies don't trust their people enough to let them be free. In some of those cases, it makes sense to push back. When I was a writer at BET, I can recall a few exchanges where producers would come to me wanting to change parts of sketches or entire concepts altogether.

On some of those occasions, I'd have to push back. "You brought me here because of my creative perspective—my style of humor, the way I write, the kind of jokes I tell. Now you're asking me not to be that person. But please, in this instance, just trust me." Just keep in mind that sometimes you win that battle, and sometimes the entire writing staff gets fired.

It was this balance of a long leash and proactive reporting that allowed Jon Werner, the CES Innovation Award winner, to create the connected soccer ball. Nobody asked his team to go create a soccer ball. There was no directive for a new kind of sporting equipment, but it resulted in this compelling product. Jon's team also developed regenerating treads on shoes, connected shoes, and apps that tell you when it's time to replace your shoes based on the number of miles you've walked.

SAY "HOW" INSTEAD OF "NO"

There's a rule in improv comedy which teaches us how

to flow within the creative process. It's often expressed as, "Yes, and…"

In collaborative exercises where two or more characters are interacting, Performer A might say something like, "Come on, Billy, let's go do some heroin!"

In the moment, Performer B cannot resist or think to himself, "No, my character wouldn't do that." Instead, Performer B might say something like, "Yes, and we'll also need two gallons of water to wash it all down."

Bad example, I know, but adopting this rule means you build onto what has been said rather than shutting that thought down and creating moments of stagnation. The same principle applies to brainstorming and idea-building.

When brainstorming, it's important to let the process be what it is and run its course no matter where it goes. Don't feel like the first thing that comes out of your mouth has to be gold. For your teams and collaborators, the brainstorm should be the safest place on earth. I should be able to spew the weirdest, uninformed notion with very little punishment for doing so. It has to be a safe place where no one ever says, "That's a stupid idea. Pack your bags, and move back home."

I always try to be a voice of reason and inclusion in brainstorms. I want everyone who has an idea to feel valued and included in the process. When it comes to brainstorming, instead of saying no to an idea, I try to figure out how we can make it work.

If someone says, "That won't work because it doesn't have scale," I might reply, "Okay, how can we give it scale?" Now we're in the flow of collaborative and creative problem solving rather than entering the room and trying to get to the right answer(s) as soon as possible.

Let's say we have a scenario where the client's response to an idea is negative, but we know it could be an extremely valuable idea for them.

Someone might say, "That's augmented reality, and we know the client doesn't like augmented reality."

Another person might respond with, "Yes, and...maybe there's a way to put it into a different context where they see the value we see."

That may lead to an exploration of how we can reposition the thought or combine it with something else.

"What if, instead of a static ad, we turned the AR experience into a live-streamed game?"

"Yes, and each user can broadcast on their social media in real time, instantly sharing with all their friends."

"Yes, and all their scores can be tracked on the website where the product is."

Now we have a combination of augmented reality, gaming, social media, and something that points back to the core business. Then we present the new idea, and despite the fact that it still includes AR, now they see how it could actually work. Hopefully. Otherwise, they might flip over the conference table and shout, "You idiots! We said no augmented reality!" So there's that possibility as well.

The point is, instead of accepting no as an answer, ask how. You might be surprised how often something valuable springs out of that one little word.

Here's another example from my family. Both my five-year-old son and my twelve-year-old daughter love making up stories. Specifically, my daughter loves scary movies like *Goosebumps*. She's seen the movie *It* four times. She started writing scary stories. I offered to write with her, so we created a shared Google Doc where we can both contribute to the story.

In one of her stories, a group of teen girls are hanging out at their friend's house. One of the girls finds out that a monster that's been terrorizing them is actually her dead grandfather who was possessed by evil spirits. Pretty morbid, I know. Obviously as a parent, my gut told me the story was too dark for a twelve-year-old. Not to mention that earlier in the story, she wrote that one of the girls was reading a magazine and smoking a cigarette.

I thought, "What does my twelve-year-old daughter know about smoking?" Instead of confronting her and asking, "You're not smoking, are you?" I made the decision to let it go. When she made spelling errors, I didn't correct her. I didn't correct the structure of the story. I decided we could fix all of that later. Instead of saying no to her, we workshopped the idea together. I concentrated on helping her get the story finished. This empowered her creativity and fostered more of it. If I had said no to any of her ideas, it would have derailed the story and shut down her creativity.

It works the same way with adults. Even if you think someone's idea is dreadful, it's still best to acknowledge their contribution in the moment and even build on it rather than deflating them. I've heard thousands of terrible concepts, and I've definitely suggested hundreds of terrible ones myself. Sometimes I'll even start by saying, "I know this is a silly notion, but hear me out..." or, "I know this concept isn't fully baked, but work with me on this..." Bad ideas often are the nuggets that lead to good ideas.

This is why I've never made anybody feel bad for their idea, even if it was way off base. In my mind, I might think, "Are you an idiot?" But I bite my tongue and respond with encouragement. In extreme cases, I might challenge the positioning of the idea instead of the idea itself. But I always ask how instead of saying no.

"How do you see that playing out? Would that happen at an event, or would that be inside the app?" When I respond that way, sometimes they turn the idea around, or they find a creative way to make it work.

The important reason to create a safe and inviting environment is that, over time, it gives individuals the opportunity to develop their creative muscles—especially for those who don't normally have the chance to participate in inventive exercises. The opposite creates and environment where nobody else wants to speak up. I've seen this happen too many times. Don't do it.

DEVELOP A THICK SKIN

There's a funny video online about office life from filmmakers Tripp and Tyler who created "The Conference Call in Real Life" video. It shows a brainstorming session where one of the team members says, "I've always wanted rain to come down in one big splash instead of individual drops over time. Think of how that could impact the irrigation system." You gotta see it.

There's a lot of truth in that video. Many times, you have a client or team member who says the craziest thing in a brainstorming session, and your job is to figure out how to make that person not feel like an imbecile. If you say, "That's the most idiotic thing I've ever heard," then you'll dampen the creative idea flow. So instead, you say something equally imbecilic like, "Maybe we can build a simulator that really makes it rain in one big splash."

However, a healthy amount of razzing is fine in brainstorming meetings as long as it's good-natured and said in a spirit of playfulness, but you can easily take it too far. A more productive solution is to use humor to redirect the group away from a truly bad suggestion. With humor, you can poke fun at somebody and they won't feel like they did something wrong—unless the joke is mean-spirited. Think of it as a low-grade comedy roast. Although those comics are ripping into each other, at the end of the day, they are the best of friends. In a safe environment, both the assailant and the victim are safe.

The truth is that 95 percent of the stuff we think of sucks or won't work. Even if it's amazing, it might not ever see the light of day for a number of different reasons. Bad timing. Not enough budget. Not enough time. Physics. The partner you wanted to work with went bankrupt. The lead person who was championing the project left the company. Murphy's Law is always in full effect.

The point is, when brainstorming, develop a thick skin. Know that some of your ideas will get shut down and that you'll make mistakes. But you can't go home with your tail tucked between your legs every time something isn't received the way you had hoped. However, I still think there's a responsibility to create that safe space where mistakes are OK.

A good friend, motivational speaker, and guest of *Innovation Crush* summed this up perfectly: "Just because you made a mistake, doesn't mean you are a mistake."

Remember the brain scan idea I mentioned in chapter 2? It was a very creative idea, we were all very proud of it, and it even got a lot of press. But it didn't quite produce the results the client expected. We had a few hiccups along the way, and I got in trouble for it. The client called me and gave me an earful on the phone call, and rightfully so, with a bunch of other people present. Luckily, doing stand-up comedy gave me really thick skin, which I needed in that moment.

Here's what happened. We had a social card that was

supposed to be generated every time someone had a brain scan. It would be emailed to you, and it was supposed to be shareable on social media. All the user had to do was click on it to share the card. But there was a glitch in the functionality, and it didn't work.

Unfortunately, we didn't learn about the glitch until the last minute, so we were trying to get it fixed. Sadly, due to a false promise by one of our partners, it did not get fixed. Meanwhile, I had to go be on a panel, so I had two other people working on it. For the client, this felt like I was being inattentive to the sudden demand.

That unpleasant experience reinforced the lessons in this chapter for me. Now, when someone says, "Wouldn't it be cool if all the rain came down in one big splash?" I reply...

"Yes! And maybe we could invent a new raincoat that people only need to wear for a few seconds. We could call it a splash coat!"

SON OF A PITCH

After all is said and done, whatever you've created has one final—and perhaps most crucial—step: the pitch.

Remember when I said we're all marketers? We're all pitching something, whether we like it or not, so get used to the idea. When it comes to investors, stakeholders, family members, collaborators, and the whole lot, gaining both their interest and trust is key.

This is one of the most underestimated and overestimated pieces of the whole innovation pie. Especially if you've created something from scratch. Formulating your crazy thoughts into digestible nuggets, visuals, and experiences is taxing. But thanks to everyone's third-grade English teacher, there's an easy rule: KISS. Keep it simple, stupid.

Personally, I like to give my creations kitschy titles. It's the first thing people usually see or hear from you and should hopefully spark some form of "That sounds interesting. What is it?" It should be simple and to the point.

- Autonomous Vehicle Game Room
- Augmented Reality Tattoo Parlor
- Alexa-Enabled Buzzfeed Quiz

You get the point. Next, it's your job to paint the picture.

I recently heard a gentleman give a speech at a school. He was deliberately unprepared and wanted to speak from the heart, but he told us a rule he learned called the Five B's: Be brief, brotha, be brief. Whether you're a brotha or not, be brief. Could you imagine if a stand-up comic took forever to get to a single punchline? You don't want to become Ferris Bueller's teacher. But therein lies a paradox since you also need to tell a story. So briefly, here are a few things to keep in mind.

INSIGHTS

Start here. What are the wow factors or things you know about the technology or consumer behavior? What anecdotes or stats or evidence do you have to back it up? What personal experience or pain point do you have? Chances are, your audience will either nod in agreement or be newly informed about an industry.

PHRASING

How you say things is often more important than what you say. I can't tell you how many times great ideas have tanked because of wordsmithery. Don't use too much industry jargon or technical terms. The famed tech writer and television host David Pogue has banked his career on speaking in way people understand. He was a guest on *Innovation Crush*, and his talk-game is lethal.

PARTICIPATION

How many of you have heard of participation? Raise your hands. See! You did it! Ask questions and get people involved. "How many of you have done a VR experience?

You in the back in the ill-fitting shirt, which one did you do? What did you like about it?"

PAY ATTENTION

I've been trained to monitor the energy in a room, positive or negative. Look for nonverbal cues, head nods, looks of confusion, drifting, note-taking, smiles, or blank stares. Use those as moments to recalibrate or continue on in the direction you're headed.

EFF IT

Nerves will always be there. Ask any seasoned comic, pitch artist, or public speaker, and they'll tell you about the butterflies they have every time they're in front of a crowd. Again, 99 percent of the things we worry about never happen, so go for it and have fun.

INSPECT THE DECK

Yes, for spelling errors and goofy mistakes. But also keep the words on the page short, pithy, and to the point. The deck is only the accent to the story you're telling. Not vice versa. Save the long-worded explanations for the appendix.

KNOW YOUR SH*T!

"Hmmm...uhhh, that's a good question. We'll get back to you on that." In my mind, I'm always playing a game when I'm pitching. I want to be smart and informed and well versed in the idea. I hate when I get stumped on a question in the room. I extra hate when it happens two or three times. Make sure you know what you're talking about through and through, and if you do "have to get back to them on that," come back quick and quadruple-informed.

STOP AT YES

"You had me at 'hello.'" When they're in, they're in. I have a client who loves volume. Any time we come with ideas, there's usually about twenty. The nos are very clear, and the yeses usually happen about four words in. As much as I want to keep stressing how awesome the idea is, I force myself to keep it moving. I know there are more in-depth pitch sessions you might have, but I've seen a number of veterans go beyond the yes and end up losing the opportunity because they talked themselves into some nexus of losing the audience.

ASSEMBLE A CAPER CREW

In the famous *Ocean's Eleven* movie series, ring leader Danny Ocean assembles a team of criminals to pull off an epic heist. Each of the different crew members has a different specialty that's essential to the team's overall success. One of the crew members is a master at sleight of hand. Another is a computer whiz. Another is a master of disguise. One team member is a contortionist. A contortionist and acrobat? What on earth would a criminal gang need with an acrobatic contortionist?

The reason Danny Ocean assembled this caper crew is that each member has a unique talent, and when they come together as a team, they can achieve incredible results.

I like the *Ocean's Eleven* parallel. The concept is to build teams with diverse and unexpected perspectives and skillsets to approach problems. Most of the time, we want to stack a design team with a bunch of engineers. I would argue that maybe the team could use a marketer in the room or an idea-smith or a writer or even a sculptor. That's your caper crew. As marketing guru Lee Clow once tweeted, "Don't say you want to create work that stands out if you insist on only hiring people who fit in."

At OMD's Ignition Factory, we typically don't hire people who have media agency experience. Instead, we create sort of a ragtag team. It's almost like in that 1980s action television series *The A-Team*, which was comprised of a bunch of mercenaries, all with different skillsets. (Note: I'm talking about the real A-Team, not that Bradley Cooper and "Rampage" Jackson crap. Although if I ever meet Rampage face-to-face, I will tell him how much I loved the film.)

First, you've got Hannibal, the organized thinker. In some cases, that's me. If I'm managing the team, I'm looking for the best ways we can use everyone's skills to solve problems. My team members are the specialists.

On *The A-Team*, you've also got Murdock, who's a little nutty but also a genius. In real life, that might be a coder or hacker tinkering away in the corner.

Then you've got Face, a handsome fellow who can do a bit

of psychological manipulation, and he's a great conversationalist and romancer. On your team, Face might be a former actor who is charming and who might be effective at pitching an idea in person. Face reminds me of a guy I once interviewed named Jeff Jenkins. He was Taco Bell's resident disruptor when I interviewed him, and he was responsible for the world-famous (among fourth-meal enthusiasts), geolocation-based Taco Bell app that would automatically place your favorite orders when you were in the proximity of a Taco Bell. Jeff was just like Face—a handsome, stylish guy who in fact once had a recurring role on the TV series *Star Trek: The Next Generation*.

You've also got Mr. T playing B.A. Baracus. He is the muscle. When you need some heavy lifting right away, he's the person who can do it. "I ain't gettin' on no plane, Hannibal." A modern-day Mr. T might be someone like former BBDO chairman and sexual behavior expert Cindy Gallop, who refers to herself as the Michael Bay of business and says, "I like to blow sh*t up."

These are close to the profiles of people you want to bring on your team. Although a bit of a metaphorical analogy, it works conceptually. You want a bunch of different people with unique skills all pulling together on the same team. Extending the comparison, the A-Team would get called in to do the missions that nobody else knew how to do. That's how I view my teams and how we should view ourselves within a group—we're a team that can get the impossible done in a creative way.

On a call I received a while back, there was a client who was trying to do something for the Olympics. If you're not a formal sponsor of the Olympics, there are thousands of restrictions on what brands can do or not do, what they can say or not say, who they can endorse or not endorse, and so on. This client needed us to help them think a bit more creatively and differently. Basically, they needed to break into the Olympics. Any commercials, technology experiences, out-of-home media buying, digital buying, banners, or anything that says "Olympics" on it is very deliberate, so we needed to find smart ways to do something notable and hack the world's biggest sporting event.

Cut to the montage of our A-Team getting to work, each team member finding unique ways to make an impact. Blueprints, maps, pictures of key people we need to avoid, the manual to the security system, the whole nine. "Here's what we know..."

The key is having a team of people who are different than you. Find people who will venture into the unknown. Their skillset, interests, and perspective are all going to be important.

One thing I've noticed a time or two after working with

dozens of start-ups is that the founding team members all seem homogeneous. They dress alike, talk alike, and act the same. That causes me some concern. Of course, you want people who share the vision and the workload, but the last thing you want in a winning team is three or four founders who are carbon copies of each other.

I have assembled a team of people from a wide variety of backgrounds: people who have created start-ups, photographers, professors, marketers, and other creatives. They each bring different tools and perspectives to the table to solve client problems in innovative ways.

I've worked with people who have written for the Netflix show *House of Cards*. I worked with one woman who worked on HBO's comedy series *Silicon Valley*, creating the fake UX design for the show's fictional apps and computer programs. I've hired a professor.

An unexpected benefit of a team like this is that you automatically stretch your own knowledge base and creative capability because you're in such close proximity to these other people's expertise. When I first started at Ignition Factory, I'd be in meetings with my team, and as we're looking for pops of culture to tap into, they'd be like, "Have you heard of this?"

"No."

"What about this?"

"Nope."

"How about this one?"

"Uhhh, lemme see...no."

With every question came new knowledge, which created a wealth of inspiration to pull from for any task. I was a bit intimidated at first because they all seemed to know so much about the world that I didn't. I thought, "Am I out of my league, here?" But I learned that was a source of diversity and strength for my team and for our clients. I just wish they would call me Hannibal.

As I've mentioned before, my team for the most part is not comprised of people with traditional media backgrounds. That creates one of the biggest learning curves when bringing new people on board. It's unfamiliar territory. It's venturing into the unknown. It's an ability to thrive in ambiguity. I find that the small amount of training required to get them up to speed is more than offset by the unique ideas they bring to the table.

SERENDIPITOUS COLLISIONS

My team is adept at doing things differently, at colliding

and making weird connections. I might come at a problem with humor; another person might come at it from a tech perspective. We had one guy on our team who brought strange scientific explanations to the table. He was part of the Earth Institute at Columbia University. He was the type of guy who understood why Apple changed the type glass on their devices long before they publicly introduced 3D Touch and other touch patterns. He actually predicted that Apple would use that same glass on the Apple Watch, and he turned out to be right. The majority of the time, I had absolutely no idea what he was talking about, but I knew it was valuable.

Having someone like that on the team created a huge learning curve, but we learned from each other. The fact that he could tell us why the glass is different on an iPhone meant I now had that perspective to add to our creative process. "Could we use the same type of functionality on a touchscreen console at a concert?" A unique perspective creates serendipitous collisions of disciplines.

You might not readily see the value in hiring somebody who doesn't immediately understand or resonate with your vision, but team members can own a specific lane. One of the guys I hired is a successful photographer. He took a two-week vacation to go on the road with a couple of bands and shoot pictures of them. He has such an artistic view of how things can look, which is something I don't have. I'm the pun-based idea guy; he's the polished photographer with the production skillset. It's a nuanced mix of disciplines and skills that allows us to approach problems from as many different angles as possible.

Taking this concept a bit more broadly, it's also good to ask people who are not on your team or in your industry for input. Let's say you built a robot; why not meet with the pastry chef down the street and get his thoughts on it?

"Hey, I'm developing this artificial intelligence. Do you understand it? What would you do with it?"

Gather different insights from people who are not swimming next to you in your lane. You'll be surprised at the insights and results that come from that.

I think it's important to hear from people who are completely outside of your team or your project. No matter how experienced or inexperienced you are, go out and seek wise council from outside experts. This is actually a biblical principle. Whether I'm working with Google Launchpad, the SXSW accelerator, the Global Entrepreneurship Summit, or talking to start-ups, I like to bring in fresh perspectives.

After receiving honest feedback, many companies pivot. They say, "We started off that way, but now we're going to do it this way." That's the point at which many companies become successful. You might be surprised how many people around you are willing to give you a listening ear.

A LESSON FROM THE L'ORÉAL INCUBATOR

Guive Balooch is a scientist-turned-cosmetics-genius who runs the Connected Beauty Incubator at L'Oréal, similar to what Jon Werner does at Adidas. Basically, Guive is an explorer. He has a team of people with a wide range of skills and talents. His team members include chemists, marketers, and psychologists, all in different locations around the world.

The core team works in the same location as Guive, but I love the fact that he is getting perspectives and disciplines from other regions and cultures. There is one team member who's in Germany, so the way that individual will look at innovations is very different from the way Guive looks at it or how someone in China might look at it. We all have our own personal and cultural references.

It's interesting to observe how different countries around the globe approach innovation and the things they create. For instance, places like China have their own Uber, a billion-dollar business called Didi, in addition to one of the largest bike-sharing programs in the world called OFO. A billion people means lots of getting from point

A to point B. I served as a judge for the CES Innovation Awards, and the conference boasts 58,000 international attendees hailing from 150 different countries. It's fertile ground for discovering how governments and cultures approach their support of start-up ecosystems, entrepreneurs, and business owners.

L'Oréal discovered a surprise in China. A couple years ago, they launched an app called Makeup Genius that got 14 million downloads in the first three months—and an unexpected 4.7 million of those came from China. Makeup Genius is an augmented reality app that allowed users to virtually try on any of L'Oréal's three hundred products. As it turns out, in China wearing makeup is a relatively new cultural norm that older generations mostly didn't do, so there's no existing tradition of girls learning from their mothers, sisters, or friends, or from their own experiments. Since previous generations didn't indulge the way we do in America, this turned out to be a great way to experiment and try different looks for droves of beauty-curious millennials and Gen Zers. It's yet another example of how having a global team with diverse cultural backgrounds can create a tool that is universally valuable, even beyond the expected markets. They probably also did not expect the selfie I took with the app (which I show at some of my talks) channeling my inner Michelle Phan and Nitraa B.

Guive is a traditional scientist with legit credentials. When he appeared on my podcast, I found an old, extranerdy scientific paper of his, and I said to him, "Just so the audience knows that you're a bona fide scientist, I'm going to read this thing, and you explain what it means. OK?"

The paper had a bunch of big, fancy, four-dollar words I didn't understand, but I read it aloud anyway. Guive laughed with me—or at me—then without missing a beat he explained exactly what it meant. He still has his chops. From a scientific and technological standpoint, he's the real deal, which is why he assembled a team of people who weren't necessarily scientists or engineers from the makeup industry. He turned L'Oréal's Connected Beauty Incubator into his own set of experiments. He had the science part handled, so he chose a wide range of superstars with vastly different specialties.

My recommendation is that you take a page from Guive. Crush the traditional box, specifically when it comes to what kind of people you hire for your projects. Be willing to take a risk and hire some odd ducks and misfit toys who at first glance might seem like they don't necessarily belong there. There is great strength in that diversity of thought.

In my own experience, I've been on both sides of the coin. When I was job-hunting on LinkedIn and Craigslist (yes, I was actually "job-hunting" and not "knob hunting"), I saw a lot of opportunities that sounded interesting, so I sent my résumé. If a person is curious enough to approach you for work even when on paper it looks like they don't belong, it's also the duty of the recipient to entertain that possibility of the candidate and see where some of his or her not-so-obvious skills might fall into play. I've seen a lot of résumés that looked weird and quirky where I said, "Let me see if there's some value here."

DON'T KILL THE PUPPETEER

If you're looking for creative problem solvers, I suggest looking beyond what you would normally be attracted to. I once tried to hire a woman who was GE application engineer working on turbines. She was moving back from Japan, where she worked doing God knows what because it's certainly out of my league. Before her move back, she had just transitioned into the sales side of the engineering process, and I figured that if she could tinker with high-functioning tech and then turn around and speak marketing and sales, she just might have a great set of skills and perspectives that could work for broader innovation work. She then introduced me to her husband, who I ended up working with later on. Such is the process of exploring someone's skills and value. New connections almost always bring unforeseen value. If you're at a networking event or your wife's uncle's brother's friend is a professional bowler or a puppeteer, there might just be something of value there.

If you've ever had the chance to sit inside an electronic puppeteering rig, you know how complicated it is. I know what you're thinking, "Of course, Chris, I do that every Saturday with my marionette meet-up group."

Whether you have or haven't, just know that it requires all ten fingers working at once. Literally every finger movement does something. One finger moves one eye, another finger moves the mouth or the right arm or determines if the puppet looks up or down, smiles, or frowns. On top of that, the performer has to voice the character while also paying attention to audience feedback, timing, and improvising live in front of kids and adults alike. It's truly fascinating to observe.

I had a chance to visit the Jim Henson Company, and they have a live digital puppetry department that allows them to project an animated image onto a screen, mount a camera on that screen, and hide the puppeteer. Then the performer manipulates the image in real time. It's basically live, interactive animation. A technology they built in the 1990s eventually created a live television series with multiple characters.

We had the thought to turn this rig into a live digital billboard experience. Imagine having a conversation in real time with the Geico lizard, Master Chief from Halo, or the rat band man himself, Chuck E. Cheese. Making it hyperpersonal, characters would be able to comment on everything from shirt colors to hairstyles to even snacks in real time.

That puppeteer analogy might sound like a joke, but talented puppeteers have many of the skills required for success in marketing. They have empathy, performance ability, timing, verbal and nonverbal communication skills, and they understand how to read and engage with an audience. Many of those skills apply in business.

So take a chance on nontraditional candidates. If you can find candidates with enough unique cultural values that fit with your organization, then those candidates are worth considering. They might turn out to be your team's Hannibal, Murdock, Faceman, or B.A. Baracus.

PUT WOMEN IN THEIR PLACE

We talked about diversity of discipline, but we can't ignore the societal angst around diversity and inclusion in regard to ethnicity and gender. The title of this chapter is about figuring out how to bring more women to the innovation table and include their voices and talents in the innovation community.

In the literal sense, General Electric CMO Linda Boff explained to me their goal to hire twenty thousand women by 2020. The company is going to great lengths to fulfill this, making great efforts to scour talent pools and deepen the pool of future female innovation mavens through STEM efforts focused on women. At the same time, this chapter is more broadly focused on the overall innovation potential of including the talents of anyone whose voice is typically underserved or underrepresented in this or any other field.

On a personal note, I signed a pledge a few years ago to not appear on any panels that do not have at least one woman on it. Since that time, a few similar movements have sparked, stemming from groups ranging from UK hyperlocal Owen Abroad and more globally recognized organizations like the United Nations. I also serve on the board of the Girls Academic Leadership Academy (GALA), California's first all-girls public STEM school.

I was interviewed at the Drum in February during Black History Month, and we had a conversation about inspirations. One of the questions was about how we can do a better job of celebrating diversity. My advice? Stop celebrating diversity.

Why am I invited to speak in February just because it's Black History Month? Why can't you call me in June? Why does an event have to program a "women's panel"? Why can't we put women on the regular ol' panel? It's a double-edged sword. Yes, you give people a platform, but you're also separating them from the rest of the group. Let's not separate people from the rest of the group based on their gender, religion, disability, skin color, or creed. Unless it's Apollo Creed. He got cocky and fought the Russians and died because of it. Don't be that guy.

I was asked to moderate a panel on the future of esports at a gaming festival. It was the *Magic Mike* of discussions.

A full-on, all-male review. Looking at the lineup weeks before the event, I brought up this issue.

"Guys, can we get a woman on this panel?"

We went back and forth talking about it for a while, and the organizers responded that they already had a women's panel. I argued that it's not the same thing.

When we were on the ground, I poked a little fun at the situation while I was moderating. Nothing better than watching a bunch of brilliant guys stammer about why everyone speaking has a penis. And yes, I actually said the word penis (gasps!)—and yes, I do know that in the population at large, a penis does not automatically mean someone is a man. But with this group, the icebreaker was used as a segue to discuss men's perspectives on the issue.

Now look, publicly I'm not the most sociopolitically active person on the planet. I'm no Jesse Williams or Jackson or the Body Ventura. But I do truly believe in the value of diverse points of view and experiences and in giving anyone their due respect and admiration. That's how I designed *Innovation Crush*. There's no *Innovation Crush for Women*, there's no *Innovation Crush Latino*, and we don't announce, "Our Mocha Soul series continues this month with Neil DeGrasse Tyson."

I keep my eyes open at all times for ways to make my show as diverse as possible. As you've probably gathered from reading this book, we've curated all types of nontraditional voices in our innovation ecosystem. Athletes, adult stars, magicians, kids, rich, poor, able-bodied or not—the colorful list of innovators goes on and on. That's what I mean when I talk about putting women in their place. It's inclusion. It's putting anyone who's done epic shit in their place right alongside the common faces we've all grown accustomed to seeing.

JOINING THE CULTURE CLUB

My brother is part of the team that runs the Detroit Economic Growth Corporation, which means his job is to bring in businesses and develop infrastructure in the city. LinkedIn recently opened some offices there, as did Microsoft, and he worked on both those projects.

My brother is very smart, and he cares deeply about the city of Detroit. At one point, the city was home to over two million citizens, which in the early 2010s had dwindled down to just over seven hundred thousand. When the mass exodus happened, he held on to his historic house for a few years. He moved out of it a few years ago, but when the city was at its worst, he weathered the storm—as any halfway-decent stock advice would instruct—staying rooted in the value he knew was inherent in the city.

One day, he mentioned to me that Detroit was working on a pitch for a major corporation to make Detroit its home. The company was looking for a place for their new center of operations, and Detroit was in the running. He went to the practice pitch meeting and said there were forty people in the room representing Detroit, but he was the only Black person. Detroit is a city that's more than 80 percent Black.

My brother was upset because he felt it was a huge missed opportunity in terms of empathy and in terms of understanding cultural needs. The whole proposal was about bringing a major company to the city by saying, "Here's what it's like. Here's what some of the needs are. Here's how we can serve you." But one of the most important cultural aspects of Detroit was not even represented in the meeting.

I was once in a room when someone pitched the thought of creating a Hispanic name generator of as part of a Latino-oriented project. The comedian in me cracked up both at the punchlines of the multihyphenated Hispanic names he rattled off and at the type of bold unawareness it took for them to say that thought out loud. I patted him on the back, jokingly course-corrected him, and enjoyed watching his face turn beet red as a newfound cultural realization washed over him.

Taking it all a step further, I know what it feels like to be in a room where I'm the HNIC (look that one up) and watch as everyone doggedly addresses another person in the room they assume is the decision maker. As a minority, you're often looked at differently. It's just a thing that's engrained in our society. Sometimes, you're not included in certain conversations because there's a preconceived notion of who belongs in the room.

FEELING ALIENATED

Everybody has experienced some form of discrimination. It's not fun, but I think that experience is more of a unifier than we realize. Maybe you're short and people don't think you're a powerful person because of it. Maybe you're tall and every other conversation is about whether or not you play basketball or volleyball. "How's the air up there, Stretch?" Maybe you're overweight or too skinny or have tattoos and piercings everywhere. We all are victims of preconceived biases that people place on us either deliberately or through genuinely not knowing an offense was made.

Now don't get me wrong, I absolutely know there is some longstanding systemic division. At the same time, there is also the universal human truth that we all feel ostracized in some way at some point in time. If you're the white dude who goes to a Black neighborhood, and you hear, "Hey, what you doing over here, white boy?"—you are now an outsider. We've all felt alienated.

That's why I like referring to innovation teams as misfit toys. It's as if many of these people have never found their tribe. I know people who have had a ton of opportunities offered to them, but they still feel lost. They get placed in areas of business they don't belong doing tasks that don't fit them, assigned by people who don't understand their capabilities. The outside world doesn't seem to understand their perspective or why they seem to meander in their career. That person might be high functioning in a specific arena, but they haven't been given the opportunity to spread their wings or the chance to truly develop their innovation muscles.

I once had a chance to meet Katherine Switzer, the first woman to run the Boston Marathon back in the 1960s. She was the first woman to do it, and she paid the price for opening the floodgates for women in the marathon business. Women runners were so uncommon, in fact, that stores didn't have shoes in the right sizes or fits made for them. The old runner dudes hated the fact that there was a woman running a marathon. A marathon, for Pete's sake! People yelled at her before, during, and after the race. What a fine display of trash talk that must've been. Can you believe that? "Get out of here, you...you...you lady!" When she actually ran the marathon, she was even physically assaulted. But like Forrest Gump, she just kept running and running. "Run, Katherine, run!"

I did an unconscious bias training in 2017, and it was one of the most mind-blowing experiences I've had. I'm Black, so of course, I go in thinking, "You people are the ones who need the training, not me! I'm the victim here!" followed by, "Maybe it's a surprise, and I'll finally get my forty acres!" (Rubs hands together in anticipation.)

Now, I consider myself a pretty open-minded individual, but I discovered that I'm much more of a jerk than I thought. In fact, we are all jerks in our own way. In one exercise, we were split into five groups, and we were given a résumé with a name on it and some background information on the person's work history. The assignment was to determine whether or not we as a group would hire the candidate. After some deliberation, each group went around the room, shared the name of their candidate, and why they did or didn't chose to hire the person.

Upon all five groups' amazing theses, (rhymes with ___), multiple rounds of point-counterpoint, and plenty of "yeah buts," the facilitator let us in on a secret: we were all given the exact same résumé. Only the names and pictures were different. Some Hispanic, some a little more Afrocentric, some Asian, and of course, a good ol' Caucasian Tom Smith to boot. It was a real eye-opening lesson about perception and reality.

The point was to uncover how we measure facts against

preconceived notions. You can stifle your own creativity if you're not open to someone else's ideas because of how they look, how they dress, something they said last week that sounded weird, or whatever petty thought about them that you've held on to—even if they're subconscious. Those judgments will get in the way of what your team is able to create because a lot of the creative process is about connecting with other human beings. And you can't fully connect with other people if you're not aware of the invisible subtleties that secretly cloud our vision.

Every major record label turned down hip-hop star Eminem, along with multiple producers. But Eminem persisted because he believed in himself and his art. Jimmy Iovine was the one who finally told Dr. Dre he needed to work with Eminem. Most people think it was Dr. Dre who took the risk, but in reality, he had the risk thrust upon him. Now Eminem is one of the most prolific artists of our time.

Sometimes we're forced to make a decision off the cuff because of life circumstances, or maybe because of a boss who forces us. Even someone we put on a pedestal like Dr. Dre was told, "You absolutely need to work with this guy." I'm sure we've all entered certain situations reluctantly and come out on top, thinking, "That was the best experience of my life. I'm glad they made me do it." Still waiting on that *Chronic* album though.

I know what some of my biases are. Do you know yours? Because I'm hoping this book will sell and people won't judge me on them, so I'll share them with you in the second book.

UNLIKE-MINDEDNESS

I believe in the idea of unlike-mindedness. Instead of having like-minded people in your caper crew who always agree with one another, look for the opposite. Actively seek out people who have contrarian viewpoints. I had one friend who would always disagree with me.

He would tell me, "No, I don't like that idea because of X, Y, and Z."

Despite his utter hater-ness, I keep going back to him because I want someone to challenge my point of view. To this day, I call him "Mikey," after the kid in the Life cereal commercials.

(Fun fact: The real Mikey is fifty years old and is SVP at a media sales company.)

(Fun bonus fact: The original commercials starred him and his two real brothers.)

Back to my friend Mikey. I highly respect him because he

has done a ton of thought-provoking work as an artist and creator. He's a filmmaker, musician, and marketer, and he has done work for Oprah, Madonna, and Deepak Chopra. He was even one of those weird people who served as a clairvoyant for police investigations. And he was successful at all of it. Thanks to an event we did together years ago, I also met my wife in part because of him. But he also had a talent for picking apart my ideas and telling me why he thought they wouldn't work.

From an innovation standpoint, he's always reinventing himself. I heard no from him so often that I got used to it, but I always sought out his opinion. I would pitch almost any random thought to him. He would say no and explain why, we'd chat about it and have a bit of a debate, and I would walk away with either a changed perspective or with the thought, "Screw that guy! I'm doing it anyway." On a rare occasion, my discussions with him led to some form of solid affirmation about whatever it is I may have been working on. That's the kind of unlike-mindedness that I think is so important. If you only surround yourself with yes-men, you're missing an opportunity to grow and become better.

Disclaimer: I never ran the idea of this book past him, but I'll be sure he gets a copy. I'm sure he'll hate it.

THE "I" IN TEAM

We need each other more than we'd like to admit. When I interviewed boxing legend Sugar Ray Leonard on *Innovation Crush*, I said, "You're an athlete, and you're held up on this pedestal as one of the best fighters ever, but tell me about your team."

He replied, "I couldn't have done any of this without a team, including a nutritionist taking the McDonald's out of my hand, a sparring partner beating me up a few times a week, a trainer, a weight coach, and so many others."

There are all of these people around celebrated innovators who make them what they are. Everyone talks about Steve Jobs, but hardly anyone mentions Steve Wozniak. Without Woz, there very well could be no iPhone. Imagine that. No one achieves greatness all on their own. When you look at the story of a successful innovator or listen to their TED Talk, you might think, "Oh, that person is a one-person powerhouse." However, that person is surrounded with other talented and dedicated people. If you deliberately cut people out because of your own personal bias, ego, or misconceptions of what success is comprised of—even though you might be unaware that you're doing it—then you do the whole personal development and creative growth process a disservice.

On the flip side, I also think it falls on the underserved

individual to do some serious door-knocking, to push hard until they get the opportunities they want. I'm not an expert in anything, so I was never the obvious, traditional choice for anyone to hire. As I told a group I was meeting with recently, my expertise is being a generalist. That makes it hard for some companies to figure out how they can use me and if they want to hire me. How did I do so many seemingly random things in my career? Often, to my own dismay, my phone is not ringing off the hook with opportunities, but one of the key reasons I wind up getting the gig is because I'm a nosy guy and I'm persistent. I knock on doors and push my way in where I know I don't readily belong. Sure, sometimes it feels like harder work, but I also get a kick out of being the unexpected surprise.

Here's another example of someone who was determined to get what she set her mind on. I know Patty Rodriguez, who produces the number one radio show in the country. Coming from humble beginnings, she was drawn to morning radio as a teen. She loved the banter, the energy, and the fact that even though we're all tucked away in our cages on wheels, we're having a universal experience by the millions. It moved her so much, one day she did something she had never done before in her young life: she lied to her mom. Patty told her mom that they had an event at school, so she needed to borrow the car. Instead of going to school, Patty drove to the local radio station and asked for a job.

Right then, she was given a job as senior vice president of programming. To everyone's astonishment she became the first female VP in the company! Yeah, right, and not quite. However, they did soon offer her an internship at the station. Back then, she barely had any life experience, let alone work experience, let alone work experience in radio. But the station manager admired her tenacity. Years later, she worked her way up, and now she's the lead producer and sometimes on-air talent for one of the most popular morning radio shows in the country.

She's also an author. As the mother to two gorgeous children, she noticed there were no bilingual books for families like hers, so she decided to start writing children's books. In my interview with her, she said she met with every major publisher, and nobody would give her a chance. One publisher even told her that Mexican women don't read books to their kids. She was not only a first-time author, but she was also dealing with biases and cultural misperceptions.

Patty wound up self-publishing her books along with her longtime friend and business partner. There's a great article featuring Patty and her book series *Lil' Libros* with a photo that shows her with stacks and stacks of boxes of books in her living room. Target, Amazon, and Barnes & Noble picked up her books nationally. Her success started and grew because Patty isn't afraid to knock on doors. Or simply kick them down altogether.

If you want to be successful, be willing to kick down some doors. There's no way around it. Go out and seize your own opportunities, especially if you're part of a traditionally underserved group or if you want something that people think is not for you.

Universally, the innovator's journey is a lonely one. When you see that the world needs a product or service or performance, chances are likely that most people will give you a blank stare, an awkward pause, and extend their hand for a "well it was nice to meet you anyway" handshake. Don't let that discourage you. Patty sure didn't.

We all want society to willingly bend to us all on its own, but until that happens, we use our will to make it bend. To me, that's a universal innovator's principle. You go out and do something that nobody else has done. Your race, color, or creed doesn't matter. Seek the opportunity, and don't take no for an answer.

DEATH BY A THOUSAND SLAPS

I'm a fan of a guy named Michael Gervais, who is an expert in high pressure performance. He says the biggest hurdle to peak performance is our self-talk. What do you say to yourself in moments of impending defeat? If something bad is about to go down, what's your self-talk? What voice do you hear in your own mind? And most importantly, what do you believe about those words? That's the difference between winning or losing in most situations.

I learned this lesson over many years of competing in martial arts. I studied martial arts for close to fifteen years. I participated in tournaments, won a few competitions here and there, and at one point, I was ranked seventh in the state of Michigan—a regular Jean-Claude Van Denson.

After chatting with Michael, I could almost replay every match I lost, realizing that my mind may not have always been as confident as my body.

Success in martial arts is a mix of positive self-talk, discipline, and trusting that you trained enough and that you're well equipped to succeed. Those things prevent a punch or a single defeat from deterring you from having a winner's mindset. It's like every Rocky Balboa movie ever. He takes in an inhumane pummeling for eleven rounds, then comes back in the twelfth to knock Mr. T upside his Mohawk to win the day. "Who pities the fool now, Adrian?" (Side note: Mr. T has an amazing Twitter feed.)

There are many similarities between martial arts and stand-up comedy—which is probably why I enjoyed each of them. Although I have to admit, there's not much that's funny about getting kicked in the face. Both require you to be fully in the moment and to know when to be defensive and when to be aggressive and confident in any situation, no matter what happens. You need to focus. You need to work on your craft. Perhaps most importantly—in both comedy and martial arts—you need to roll with the punches, take your lumps, not get discouraged, and constantly overcome small failures.

In business, it's pretty much the same thing. I call the day-to-day failures that we all experience "microfailures."

One or two microfailures is no big deal, but if a bunch of them start to pile up, it can be devastating.

Just like in martial arts, most matches are not won or lost by a single, powerful, knockout blow. Rather, matches are most often won or lost by dozens of smaller blows that wear you down and drain your energy. I think failure works the same way for most people. Most people don't have one spectacular failure, they have hundreds and hundreds of smaller failures. I call it "death by a thousand slaps."

WHEN MICROFAILURES PILE UP

I haven't built a ten-million-dollar company, then lost all the money and had to move back into a one-bedroom apartment. I haven't had a grand failure like the ones we hear about in keynotes and articles and in the back alleys of Silicon Valley. What I've had are hundreds of microfailures, the seemingly little things that stack up and start to feel like one giant failure. It's not necessarily the same way that people normally talk about it, but the effect can be the same. We don't talk enough about the little failures, the slaps that sting in isolation.

Sometimes a microfailure is sending out twenty unreturned emails. Sometimes it's being denied a meeting that you really want. Sometimes it's having your ideas shot down in a pitch meeting. As in innovator, microfailures are the things that make you feel disheartened about the process of bringing your ideas to fruition.

We've all had times where a bunch of microfailures happen all at once, even outside of work. Maybe your kid's not doing well in school. You don't get invited to an industry event or conference. You lose a deal to a competitor. Your funding gets cut, or one of your star employees decides to quit. Any of these microfailures can take you out of that place of exploration for a short while or for a very long time if you let it.

Another fascinating person I had on *Innovation Crush* twice is Jason Mayden, formerly the senior global design director for Nike's Brand Jordan. Jason talked about how he left Nike to launch his own fitness and apparel brand for kids called Super Heroic. Weeks before the launch of his business, which was backed by several entrepreneurs, including Irving "Magic" Johnson, Jason's laptop was stolen. Along with all his design files. And his corporate documents. And, of course, his calm spirit.

Jason had to return to good old-fashioned pencil and paper for his next round of designs before his launch. A daunting exercise to say the least, but a hidden gem in returning to his design roots. His launch has been amazingly successful. I don't know about you, but we're ransacking the whole house if I can't find my keys in the morning, let alone my computer that contains everything I've worked on for the last two years.

FAIL HARD AND FAIL FAST? NO THANKS

I think we overglorify the idea of failure in this country. There's a belief that if you must fail, you should fail hard, fail big, and fail fast. Many people say if you're not failing, you're not innovating. There's a lot of lore and legend that failing is somehow admirable and noble.

The truth is, nobody wants to fail. No inventor out there is like, "Let me go blow this investment on thousands of mistakes!" Similarly, when you get married, you don't expect things to not go well. Most divorces don't happen over some epic, life-changing disappointment. It's several small moments that add up to "You know what? I'm out." If you do wind up divorced (either from your spouse, or your project/job), it's tempting to think you didn't do the relationship right and caused it to fail. Don't play that game. The goal should always be to win—and like we've heard thousands of times, learn something from it.

When it comes to business, the innovator is often the first into the fray, so when we experience a setback—or a slew of them—it feels like we're all alone. There's no blueprint on how to recover from your particular type of failure. Sometimes the microfailure is just waiting for your idea or business to catch on. You keep pitching and building and emailing and meeting and tweaking and doing all the right things. You're supposed to build the momentum by doing all of this work up front in hopes that it will pay off. It's like the snowball effect gone all wrong. The more you push it, the bigger and heavier it gets, amassing potential resources, opportunities, hiccups, and even accolades. And somehow, it's not yet rolling on its own, becoming harder for you to push. It can begin to feel discouraging after a while, and even that angsty feeling is a form of failure. You begin to become more sensitive to the series of small disappointments.

Most of us experience this feeling in isolation. We think we're the only one dealing with all of these microfailures, but the truth of the matter is that it's far more common than we give it credit for—especially in an era of social media where we are constantly flooded by other people's images and anecdotes of success.

"New boots!"

"Signed that deal today!"

"Just closed on my $300 million exit."

"KFC sent me this free bucket of chicken in the mail today. #ColonelSwag"

(Fun fact: KFC literally follows eleven herbs and spices on Twitter.)

So what do you do? I encourage you to open up to a mentor or a friend. Have some honest dialogue, and you'll find that you are not the only one who's experiencing those feelings. Your specific circumstances might be unique, but the emotional experience stemming from series of slaps is similar to what others also experience. Microfailures, when they occur in isolation one after another, can break down your creative spirit.

Everyone can recall a period of time when a bunch of microfailures all stacked up. The car broke down, the kid got sick, you lost a big client, and your landlord increased your rent all on the same day. One thing after another. If feels awful. Your stress level skyrockets; you want to tear that "Hang in there" kitty poster down in an epic fashion.

There was somebody I knew who wanted to get hired on a project with me, and I had to tell him that I didn't have a role for him more than a few times. He was disappointed, almost to the point of lashing out at me. After we talked about it, it turned out he was mostly frustrated because he'd been trying to do a series of creative projects and hadn't been able to get any of them off the ground. Plus, he had a break up. Plus, one of his business partners had moved on. Not working on my project was one more microdisappointment in a long line. As friends, we were able to talk it out and address the bigger picture.

There are many ways that microfailures can manifest, not only in the business world but in life in general. One thing affects another. Keep moving forward. Positive self-talk is really powerful in those moments.

RIGHT THING, WRONG TIME

Recently, I was asked to put together an idea for a global arts program for a Fortune 50 company. It was a gigantic assignment. Build it from the ground up, invent it the way we wanted to invent it, and truly empower everyone involved, including artists and arts communities around the world. That is my favorite kind of project. A blank canvas. Reimagine. Impact. Do cool shit.

But sometimes a huge blessing can also be a microfailure in and of itself.

While on the surface it was amazing, taking this on would also mean that, to an extent, we'd have to ignore everything else we had been working on. This big new assignment quickly dominated our schedules and took priority over everything else, including personal and family activities.

Suddenly, my team and I were thrust into an awesome

opportunity, and everything else got put on the back burner. When that happens, you run the risk of losing some other opportunities, missing some deadlines, or skipping an important set of tasks because of the chaos. We had no choice but to focus on the biggest opportunity and work like crazy to try to keep all the other projects going, too. It was brutal, but we pulled it off.

Right now, you might be juggling a few different things. It's not easy. Being malleable and bending to the process can suck, even when the opportunity is great. The client was pleased, and everything about the project was awesome—except for the fact that I had to ignore everything else that was going on in my life. Sometimes the blessing can become a series of failures in spite of itself.

Other times, it's just Murphy's Law in full effect. Good things happening at the wrong time is one thing, but there is definitely never a good time for bad things. "Boy, I'm glad Grandma died on Friday and not on Tuesday," said no one ever. An inconvenience is an inconvenience. Not that I'm downgrading your grandma's passing (bless up) to a mere inconvenience, but you get what I mean.

When you're trying to manage a dozen things, it can feel completely overwhelming, especially when one of the things you're juggling suddenly needs all of your attention. You can't drop eleven other responsibilities to focus on one, so you wind up having many sleepless nights. Everything becomes inconvenient, and physically, you don't get enough rest.

There's a quote I like from a neuroscientist named Moran Cerf who was on my show once. He asked me, "Do you know what the number one cause of happiness is?"

"A bump of cocaine?"

"The number one cause of happiness is sleep."

Scientifically, that's the number one cause. It's not family. It's not sex. It is sleep. Almost everything else is outside stimuli. Your body and mind need recovery in order to process anything and everything in a sound manner. When you're burning the midnight oil, you're doing so at the risk of lots of consequences.

The money you finally make won't make you happy if you become exhausted in the process of earning it, your body tanks, and you have a heart attack. Giving your body a break is a great refresher.

With the big assignment, it wasn't that the whole business was going to collapse from the weight of it all, but any of my other tasks could have failed—and potentially my sense of wellness along with it. But these things do happen.

Prepare yourself for a few sleepless nights. Catnap in the car. Take a five-minute mental break. Will you still be able to perform to the best of your ability? You know some things will slip through the cracks, but miracles usually find a way into our situations, or we find a way to make miracles happen.

YOU ARE MICRO-AWESOME

In *The Power of Now*, Eckhart Tolle says that at any given time, we are two people. "On one hand, you're the person having the experience, and on the other hand, you're the person observing the person having the experience."

During those times where everything is going crazy, part of you is absolutely positive that you'll be OK. However, the more of a calamity we seem to enter, the quieter that second person gets. Acknowledge that these microfailures are happening and that they're taking a toll, and know that you'll be OK.

Conversely, we often forget to celebrate our wins. I happened to interview Coach Harlan Barnett of Michigan State University shortly after their one-hundredth Rose Bowl win a few years ago.

When asked what the key to their success was during

the season, he said, "No matter how small the win, we celebrated it."

From showing up on time to getting good grades to scoring a touchdown to getting both shoes on the right feet, they got in the habit of finding wonder and success in life's seemingly mundane little victories.

To this day when I have my weekly team meetings, I ask, "What were your two wins from last week, and what is a hurdle for this upcoming week?" There have definitely been times where I've felt like there were no wins at all! But being forced to present a few to a small group gets you recalibrated and focused on the good stuff.

We tend to forget that we are pretty awesome individuals. You've survived a lot in your life, maybe something as extreme as cancer, or maybe the fact that you finished a proposal in the nick of time. On the way to Art Basel in Miami, my power supply almost comedically would not stay in the plane's outlet. I was like Mr. Bean as I repeatedly tried to plug it back in. After the fifteenth attempt, and two annoyed passengers later, my laptop finally died. I was not able to finish my presentation for the next day. Upon landing, I was up half the night and finished putting together a talk at 7:15 a.m. for a breakfast presentation at 8:00 a.m. In my mind, it was a win! I even had time to go over to Starbucks, grab a coffee, give a high five to two meth heads (it is Florida, after all), kiss a random baby, and get back to the venue with twenty minutes to spare. And my delirium? It just made me a little more crazy-weird-fun than my usual self.

We forget how well we've performed in the past or the things we've overcome, so we need—and deserve, quite frankly—an ongoing combination of celebrating ourselves, basking in our microvictories, and motivating our teams. It sounds biblical, but in those moment of angst when you're feeling overwhelmed, remind yourself that this too shall pass. No matter how stressed you are, remind yourself it won't be like this forever, even if it feels like it.

Stay focused and do what you can, knowing that you can't fix every problem immediately. I sometimes read emails and then respond to them later, especially when it's an urgent or angry email that says, "We didn't get our widgets on Tuesday!" Seems counterintuitive since many of us would respond right away, but I sometimes wait even a few hours or a day before I respond. I want time to go ask questions or investigate first. There have been times when I started to write emails, then paused and started over. The first response was whatever was on my mind, but I had to take a breath and remember to be thorough, both on and off the email thread. At the very least, I might say, "Let me look into this."

Also, when did widgets become the industry standard example product? Why not socks? Or bolts? I love bolts.

GET OVER YOURSELF

Keeping your eye on the ball is a little cliché. I think it's more about getting through it than it is taking your eye off the ball. As innovators, we don't necessarily take our eye off the ball. Instead, we keep reminding ourselves not to get emotionally derailed by failures and problems.

Shira Lazar is an award-winning journalist who hosts a show called *What's Trending*. In its earliest iteration, it was exactly what it sounds like. "Here's what's next in society, media, and technology that you guys should know about." Over the years, it shifted more toward influencer culture, what's happening online, and who's doing what in the online arena.

Shortly after Shira started *What's Trending*, she had a deal with a major television network. She and her company were banking their success on it. At the eleventh hour, after months of work, the deal fell apart. That was more than a microfailure, and Shira went through a period of time where she was depressed. She was curled up on her bedroom floor for days. And she felt as though she couldn't move on to the next thing.

She even felt doubly bad because she knew better than

to let this setback get her down. I know I've been there, not only upset about what went wrong, but upset that I'm upset about what went wrong. Eckhart Tolle would've hated me.

Shira had put her blood, sweat, and now tears into this opportunity only to have it fall through. Eventually, she had to pull herself out of that feeling, recalibrate, reconfigure, and get back in the taking-her-destiny-into-her-own-hands mentality. Her show is now an international sensation, boasting a ton of partnerships with media networks in other countries and on other platforms like YouTube, live.ly, and Gas Station TV. Yes, you've probably seen her while pumping your gas, right in between Jimmy Fallon and your local news. She didn't start another business. She found another avenue for *What's Trending*, and she believed that maybe the network show didn't happen for a reason.

Every no gets you closer to a yes. You might often feel like that's a bunch of horse hockey, but I believe it's true. You know what you want, and when it doesn't happen, that sucks. However, the idea is to keep innovating and planning. If you believe in the product enough, keep trying. The one thing that might get you through it is an excited belief in the product you're making. Shira knew that *What's Trending* was a winning concept, so she stuck to it when most other people would have quit.

BACK TO THE BUMPS

There are good ideas that are smart and fun and clever and will probably even win over a crowd on any given day. Then there are the ones that give you goosebumps. The thought of them makes the hairs on your arm stand up. It makes you smile like after you've left an amazing first date and received the perfect closing text message on top of it.

On our whiteboard, we might have a dozen ideas, but only one or two of those will be goosebump ideas. I'm not a psychologist, but I imagine that having a strong physiological response to an idea means you're connected and committed. This is the kind of connection you need to survive the bumps and the bruises you'll experience along your innovation journey. If Shira had only thought *What's Trending* was kind of a cool idea, then when the network lost interest in it, she would have gone back and done something else. But it was a goosebump idea for her.

As she stated during our chat, "I think it's more that I was sick of waiting around for someone to give me permission to do what I love doing."

You can only do that with the ideas you really love—the must-have ideas. There are the nice-to-have ideas, and then there are the absolutely must-have ideas that you're most passionate about. Those are the ones that will get you to keep moving past any failure.

FLEE LIKE A REFUGEE

What are you willing to risk for your success? It's a matter of risk versus reward. Let me explain with an extreme example.

One guest on my show, Bassem Youssef, risked everything. Including his life. Bassem is a famous television host who has been called the Jon Stewart of Egypt. He even appeared on *The Daily Show* a few times as a guest, but he had his own version of *The Daily Show* called *Al-Bernameg* in Egypt. Originally, he was a heart and lung surgeon. After seeing political violence and atrocities in his home country, he grew tired of giving people medical attention out in the streets because of them. Bassem started a vlog on YouTube to comment on the situation, share how he felt about the government, and discuss events that were happening. As one of the first in the region on YouTube, that vlog grew in popularity and eventually became a TV show with over sixteen million weekly viewers. To put that in perspective, Jon Stewart at his peak had around three million weekly viewers.

Bassem launched a new career as an Egyptian political satirist talking about serious issues, and he gained a massive audience. Political satire in Egypt isn't protected speech like *The Daily Show* here, where the worst thing that can happen is a sitting United States president insults you with a 3:00 a.m. tweet. In Egypt, there was a very real risk of danger, imprisonment, or worse for people who criticized certain political factions.

Tickling Giants is a recent documentary about Bassem's journey, and how he spawned a new political movement in that country. I asked him about one scene in the film where a girl walks into the production office and says, "Guys, it's getting hectic out there. If you want to work from home today, that's fine." They were making a comedy show, and it was so dangerous to be on the job that they didn't feel safe. Meanwhile, my jokes barely get an eye roll, let alone put me in harm's way. For many Americans, that's hard to grasp. But in Bassem's world, the risk was insane.

Bassem produced his show under extreme conditions with legitimate threats to his livelihood and safety. Not only that, he became the victim of frivolous lawsuits designed to harass and intimidate him. The lawsuits meant that he could either have been arrested and thrown in jail or be buried in legal fees.

Ultimately, when he felt the risk was too much, he decided to leave the show behind. There were several indicators along the way that this was becoming too dangerous of an endeavor. He was putting his life at risk, his team at risk, his family, his children, everything. He made the decision to move to Canada and later to Los Angeles, where he lives now.

Here in the freedom of the United States, Bassem has been in the process of reinventing himself. He has the same sociopolitical point of view on the world and the same comedic approach to things, but he's planning his second chapter. Plus, he's one of the coolest vegans I've ever met.

When I talk about fleeing like a refugee, the title of this chapter, Bassem's story put it into perspective. Whatever you're trying to do probably isn't anywhere near as risky or downright dangerous as what Bassem was doing in Egypt. Whatever you're trying to build, you're most likely not facing imminent danger. I can't imagine you receiving death threats for that photo editing app you developed.

"Honey, they're coming for the app. Listen to me. You

and the kids have to get out of town now! Remember that place we went to for our anniversary and I had the idea for the app? I'll meet you there. I love you. Stay strong."

Any risks that we Americans take as aspiring creatives, artists, politicians, or entrepreneurs pale in comparison to what Bassem lived through.

How much risk are you willing to take? What's a healthy risk? Often, the risks we have in our head are based on fear—they're more the perception of risk than reality.

LEARN TO LIKE RAMEN NOODLES

What's a real risk versus just feeling nervous or uncomfortable? How bad is it really to hit rock bottom, and are you willing to risk it in order to achieve your goals? Can some of it be alleviated by everything my mom has been trying to tell me since I was fifteen?

When I speak at colleges, they often want to know the best career advice I can give. My answer is almost always, "Be smart with money." That has nothing to do with your résumé, your job, or your network. If you lose your job tomorrow or your whole department is let go or the company goes under altogether, the next job you more than likely get will probably be something you take because you need the money, not something you feel emotionally connected to. But if you are smart with your money and have a financial safety net in place, you can probably wait for the right career opportunity instead of jumping on the first one that that comes along.

TV host and celebrity chef Anthony Bourdain often talks about how he didn't even have a savings account even though he had a bestselling book and a popular TV show. In his own words, he had no safety net. That's a risky way to live, even for a celebrity. A safety net can mitigate all kinds of risk, especially career and job risk. As I tell those college students, the most important thing for your career is not making sure your résumé is polished, or that you're pitching yourself in multiple places. It's being smart with money. Stay debt-free and build up a safety net. It gives you more options.

As you're pursuing your vision, you will probably need to convince others to take risks with you. Many entrepreneurs must convince talented team members and collaborators to work for less money or leave whatever sure thing they're already doing in order to be a part of something great. If you take a family-and-friends round of investment, they're taking a risk along with you as well. Even when it comes to your immediate family, you're risking your mortgage and food on the table. Obviously, there are varying levels of extreme, but every action has potential consequences, good and bad.

To assess your risk threshold, ask yourself some hard questions. Are you willing to leave your job to focus on your idea? Are you willing to eat ramen noodles for a year in order to chase your dream? Or are you someone who needs a platinum American Express company card and expense account? Will your husband or wife be able to handle your late nights and audacious dreams? Are you an intrapreneur—an entrepreneur who happens to work within a larger company—who will fight the good fight for as long as it takes?

Do some soul-searching to determine the level of risk you will accept. At the same time, know that the world is flexible and you can design your vision around your lifestyle. In other words, you can innovate your own processes and plans. There is always a way—you just have to innovate it. You're only as limited as you believe you are.

ISUZU RODEO DREAMS

Sometimes, regardless of the risks involved, you must take the plunge and chase your dream. When I decided to create my own agency, I was working at the American Film Institute. I had recently proposed to my wife, and then about a month later, I sat her down and told her, "I want to quit my job and start my own company."

She replied, "Really?"

"Yup! See, I tricked you into committing to me, then I flipped the whole game on you!"

I forged ahead and founded Genius Effect Media Group. The agency did OK but not great. Although we did some great projects for the likes of Sony Pictures, the Venice Biennale, George Soros, and tons of small- to medium-sized businesses, it wasn't the grand slam I hoped it would be. It was a constant fluctuation between feast (yay!) and famine (boo!). We had no shortage of rough patches, but I eventually recovered from the risk of leaving a high-paying job.

Long before Genius Effect, the first time I made a major leap into the unknown was when I decided to move from Michigan to California. I made the decision because that guy from the TV network told me to "come back during pilot season." Aside from my best friend, he was the only person I had met in Los Angeles who actually lived in Los Angeles. I was thrilled by the invitation even though I knew it was loosey-goosey, at best. I packed all of my stuff into my Isuzu Rodeo and drove across the country for thirty-six hours, dreams of television comedy stardom in my eyes the whole way.

When I arrived, I rented a small studio apartment that was the same price as my two-bedroom apartment in Michigan. I rented it sight unseen because it was right next door to my best friend. We literally shared a wall. I couldn't go and visit ahead of time, so I made the deposit on a whim and took a chance.

I left Michigan on Mother's Day—a story to this day that my mom very much enjoys telling. I wanted to get on the road early on a Sunday so I could drive straight through with less traffic for a majority of the trip. My mother remembers standing on the front steps as I backed out the driveway, making eye contact and waving. She cried her eyes out while mine filled with hope. I slowly rolled on to a new future.

Then I crashed into the mailbox.

Just kidding, but that would've been funny.

I think that kind of move is easier when you're by yourself and twenty-two. The stakes are different when you're thirty-two or forty-two. Risk came knocking on my door when my daughter was born at age twenty-nine. (She wasn't twenty-nine. I was. That would've been weird, though.) It was a grueling process because, at the time, I had lost a job. I was managing an apartment building for a real estate company but was let go when the new owners came in with their own caper crew, and I wound up couch-bouncing. Her mom and I were sharing custody, so I spent time living out of my car and staying at friends' houses in between visits. I had one friend who had an extra studio apartment in Van Nuys, so I stayed there for a while. I had a mattress on the floor and a playpen, and that was pretty much it. Living the dream.

That was the closest I had ever gotten to considering a move back to Detroit. I was not living the life I had expected. When I left my hometown, I didn't expect to become a single parent. I grew up in the Midwest, and I still had those Midwestern values. I was the youngest child and, family-wise, had a lot to live up to and overcome. The weight of the world was on me.

Ultimately, I wound up staying in LA, and I've never lived anywhere else. At the time of consideration though, part of me thought that if I hadn't achieved any stability by that point, I never would. I had already been a writer, an actor, and a producer. I started a DJ business, gotten my real estate license, produced events, promoted clubs and then some—all in hopes that this snowball would continue to gain some momentum. I had dreams of living in a condo on the beach and selling my own TV series, but my reality was looking more and more like I would soon be back in Detroit, living in my mom's basement and working second shift at Applebee's. That was the risk I was dealing with.

As the pendulum started to swing back in my favor career-wise, my daughter began to live with me full time. That also gave me a renewed focus and energy and pride, and also a little bit of nervous poop in my pants. I remembered seeing her walk for the first time in that studio apartment with its air mattress and playpen. It sounds heart-wrenching, but I knew there was success around the corner, I just didn't know which corner—although I'm pretty sure I was parked on it a few nights and got a ticket.

I was holding out for a turning point. Maybe it was stubbornness or hardheadedness, or maybe it was ego. There are a number of reasons why I didn't give up and go home. It was probably the same for Bassem Youssef. I'm sure there were multiple points where he considered shutting down his show, but he had a greater mission. He was giving power back to the people. He was changing the world. Even though I may not have been able to fully articulate it at the time, my mission became to empower people by helping them increase their innovation potential.

Later in life, I learned a phrase that I adopted once things started to get better for me. It goes like this: "Sometimes God puts you through things so you can tell someone else how you got through them." That difficult part of my journey has helped me advise many people I know who are dealing with a plethora of different life issues.

WHAT WE ALL HAVE IN COMMON

The same thing happens on any entrepreneurial or innovation journey. This book isn't like a TED Talk or PowerPoint presentation with some millionaire CEO up on stage bragging about how successful she's become. In fact, it's the opposite; I still feel like I'm not there yet, and I use that feeling as motivation to continue striving for new plateaus. In this book I'm showing you how hard this journey can be, how much time it takes, and what rock bottom can sometimes look like. But who knows, maybe you're on the serendipity train and everything is chugging along smoothly. Even still, hopefully some of this becomes a tool you'll go back to if you ever hit a rough patch.

In his book, Sugar Ray Leonard discusses how he was molested as a youth. Shira Lazar almost lost everything she built and got so depressed she couldn't leave the house. Bassem Youssef had to leave his country. Patty Rodriguez cherished the truth but lied to her mom. Andrew McGregor became numb to the world while trying to help kids. Daymond John, the famed *Shark Tank* entrepreneur, and a guest on *Innovation Crush*, mortgaged his mom's house twice and lost it both times while starting his clothing line FUBU. What we all have in common is that we have opportunities to calculate and take risks. Many times, these risks come back to bite us in the butt. But in order to achieve, you have to stick with it. You have to hang in there and keep trying.

Of course, not everything you do is going to be as risky as what Bassem went through. Not everything is going to be as risky as when I moved across the country. Sometimes, the risk is deciding which project to work on or which aspect of a project to work on for a particular day. Decisions themselves are like dominoes; each one affects the ones that come after it. Should I work on the marketing of the product today or on the product itself? Do I skip dinner tonight with my family, or do I tell my client I need another day? Should I work on the branding, or should I hire someone to do it? Do we pivot the business now or wait it out? These kinds of decisions all involve risk. Risk is part of everyday life, so get comfortable with it.

THERE'S NO WRONG ANSWER

What we do in any given moment presents risk. I read a Wayne Dyer quote a while back that gave me some comfort. He said, "The universe is like a GPS. Even if you make a wrong turn, the universe will course-correct to get you to where you're going." In other words, whether you choose to go left or right, there's essentially no wrong answer. Do what you can do, make the best decision you can make at the time, and let the pieces start to fall into place. The worst that will happen is you need to recalibrate.

Achieving the right balance is key. Determine how much risk is acceptable and how much is too much, but know that you have more power than you think you do. When it comes to perceived risk, it might not be as bad as you make it out to be. Remember, 99 percent of the things you worry about don't happen.

NO MO' FOMO

I think FOMO, the Fear of Missing Out, is real. Not to be confused with mofo, which Urban Dictionary describes as "One who is hard-core." For instance, you're almost finished reading this book, which makes you one bad mofo! But FOMO is not merely a social media construct. It's a part of life. Every decision and action takes away time from other possible decisions and actions and can often leave us with a quagmire. "If I do X, then I may not get to do Y and Z." This is the kind of leap innovators have to make. Play out the scenarios of different options and see where the greatest likelihood of success lies.

In life and in business, there's always a decision to make. I say to most of my podcast guests at some point, "You've had many opportunities in front of you, some related directly to what you're building. Some are directly related to who you are as an individual. Some just may sound cool and exciting. How do you decide which opportunities you're going to pursue?"

When you hear about a company or an individual that

does fifty different things, all of them housed under a single umbrella, you wonder what they turned away. I was talking about Kevin Hart at lunch the other day. He has a shoe company, he launched a comedy platform, he's done multiple movies, and he has a minor league sports team—and that's just the tip of the iceberg of the Kevin Hartmobile. How does he filter all of the potential opportunities to decide which ones he's going after? Is it money? Is it the chance to diversify? Is it just something that's purely awesome? Is it a favor to a friend? Some long-lost childhood dream?

I think, ultimately, there's no easy answer to the quagmires we often face. There are planned circumstances, and then there are opportunistic circumstances. Sometimes an opportunity takes years to develop; other times an unmistakable opportunity falls squarely in your lap out of the blue. The latter is more fun, but each has its benefits. The truth is, nobody knows the right or wrong answer. No one can predict the future. Try and test and learn and do what you can. Make the best decision you can based on the information you have at that moment, and then ride it as far as you can.

HOLD ON TO YOUR BUTTS!

When it comes to innovation, there's no universal winning formula. Take your best guess. If you're inventing something, go for it. Try your best, put everything into it, and hope to goodness it works. There are always opportunities to learn, so treat every decision like a test and learn from the consequences. Remember that nothing is final. After you go through all the principles in this book, you'll see that reinvention isn't only the product or service you're creating. It's also the process you go through, both internally and externally, to make it happen.

In the first *Jurassic Park* film, the protagonists are trying to reengineer the security system to keep themselves protected. Time is running out, people have died already, and the dinosaurs are on their way. Their solution isn't quite ready or fully fleshed out, which is basically to shut down the system and turn it back on to reboot the computers. Just before hitting the fourth and final switch, Sam Jackson utters, "Hold on to your butts!"

We've all been there, holding on to our butts as we take a leap of faith.

RUIN EVERYTHING

I'm a huge fan of Adam Conover and his show *Adam Ruins Everything* on truTV. I 1,000 percent geeked out when he came on to *Innovation Crush*. In every episode, Adam debunks a pillar of our society. It might be weddings, funerals, science, the economy, shopping malls, or the suburbs. Virtually no topic is off limits. What Adam does is basically rip apart what you think you know about these subjects by going right to the source and presenting little known facts and information that contradict what we all thought we knew. It's enlightening.

Each episode of his show starts with somebody celebrating something, and then Adam pops up in the scene, and the actor says to him, "Oh, no, are you going to ruin this, too?" He told me that in real life, that's kind of who he is. Even in a world where every debate is settled by taking ten paces and pulling out your cell phone, Adam's the annoyingly endearing guy at a party who will tell people the real facts about a specific topic. He's learned to turn it into comedy and entertainment. Be the annoying bug in the room, the gnat in everybody's ear, to force people to entertain what you're saying.

For instance, in his episode about the suburbs, Adam talked about the fact that the suburbs were originally presented as an opportunity for people to achieve the American dream. But really, he explains, suburbs came about as a result of systemic racism. Watch the episode and you'll see how he arrived at that theory.

In the episode on shopping malls, Adam talks about how much things cost when you go into a retail store, how malls were first designed, and things of that nature. He also discusses little-known facts about how one company basically monopolizes the entire eyeglasses ecosystem. They own almost all the sunglasses manufacturers, the lens makers, the frame makers, the optometry facilities, and the insurance companies that measure and prescribe lenses. So whether you're wearing Coke bottle glasses or Ray-Bans, they control how you see, what you see, and how much it'll cost you to see. It really makes you think about how much choice we think we have versus how much we actually have.

My interview with Adam was cool from an innovation

perspective. Raised by scientists, he questions reality by always asking, "Is it really what we think it is?" He digs deeper to find out why things are the way they are. What if we used his use his methodology on the cultural gravitation toward social media. Is it because we get to show pictures, pretend to be other people, and be voyeurs? Or is it about psychological acknowledgment? Was social media originally built as a government tool so the government could monitor data on individuals? Adam explores all of these questions. By the end, the viewer has learned that things are not always as we thought—and that the best way to find out the truth is by asking those insightful questions.

The power of Adam's show is that he tears apart conventional thinking. He wants to change the way we look at things, and then the things that we look at will begin to change. Adam is the epitome of that. He deals with stuff that seems fairly mundane until you dig deeper. He's done it time and time again. Voting. Halloween. Summer break. Hospitals. Weddings.

BE A TRUTH EXPLORER

The key concept in *Adam Ruins Everything* is that you must understand the truth of why certain things exist in order to truly change them. That's how new perspectives emerge. This is especially true when it comes to innovators. The power of innovation comes from questioning things. Questions are powerful. Albert Einstein once said, "If you gave me twenty-four hours to save the world, I'd spend twenty-three of them asking questions." (Side note: There sure are a lot of Einstein quotes. I can't tell if ol' Albert just talked all the time or actually did real sciencing. Thanks, internet, for another bottomless pit of information despair. SMH.)

But most people skip the questions. Instead, they dive right into the solution. When most people approach a problem or have an idea, they tend to jump right in to the doing part rather than continuing to learn and explore more about the problem by asking questions.

When you ask questions, you get a deeper understanding of the potential and the possibilities. "We didn't even think about that." Force yourself to become an explorer of real truth. Real truth recognizes that your subject is ever-evolving. You don't know the full story yet. Keep asking questions until you do.

I admire people who continue to question things, even when everyone else believes them to be true. Consider that much of what we believe to be hard science is still theoretical. Every year, hundreds of things we thought to be absolutes are not. Even poor little Pluto got voted off the intergalactic planetary reality show. That's why the Flat-Earthers are coming back. From an innovation standpoint, consider the possibility—even if just for the fun or the sake of creative expansion—that the weird theories might be right.

Many investors heard Jeff Bezos's pitch for Amazon.com in the early days. They saw his vision and skeptically thought, "You're going to sell books online? Really?" But Bezos had done his research and asked all the right questions. He looked at the retail numbers for books; he looked at mail orders (not brides). He knew that compared to other products like clothing or kitchen supplies, books were the number one items ordered, and there are hundreds of thousands of products in that category. Meanwhile, brick-and-mortar bookstores can only stock a few thousand titles at a time. He saw the opportunity and committed to it even when nobody believed him.

Bezos questioned the need for going to a bookstore. "Do you really need to go into a bookstore to buy a book?"

Barnes & Noble scoffed at him. "Of course you do."

A couple of retailers even tried to sue him. That's what happens when you ask an annoying question.

CHALLENGE CONVENTION

Breaking the four-minute mile is one of my favorite stories. Back in the 1940s, everyone thought it was humanly impossible to run a mile in less than four minutes. Then Roger Bannister questioned that reality, believed he could do it, and broke the record. He wasn't even a professional runner. He had minimal training and was practicing as a junior doctor at the time. Suddenly, something that everyone thought was scientifically impossible became possible. His record only lasted forty-six days. Within a few years, the four-minute mile was so common, it almost became an average time for elite runners around the world.

True innovation starts with asking questions that challenge convention. You might not have some big epiphany of an idea in your head already, but through questioning and considering convention, you'll be surprised at what you uncover.

"Is there a better way to do this? Why can't we do it this way? Why has it always been done the same old way?"

Whether deliberately or incidentally, innovators innately ask questions that break the rules. The founders of car-sharing service Uber asked, "How can we leverage all that underutilized transportation capacity in privately owned cars? Why can't an everyday citizen be a taxi driver?"

Back before Uber, those questions sounded ridiculous. As a potential Uber driver, most people thought, "I don't want to be a taxi." But then they realized, "Oh, I can make some money while I drive."

I got in an Uber at 8:00 a.m. The driver had been working since 7:00 a.m. He told me that he planned to head to his regular job later. For him, Uber was a way to make additional income to supplement his salary while being out and about and meeting people. For others, it's a full-time means of being entrepreneurial. In Texas, I rode with a deaf driver who used an iPad and keyboard to communicate with his passengers. Neither Steve Jobs nor Travis Kalanick could've predicted this. This is only possible because someone dared to ask, "Would car owners be willing to chauffer around complete strangers if they got paid to do it?"

Similarly, Airbnb asked, "Why can't people turn their homes into hotels?" Getting in the habit of asking questions that challenge convention is the key. It's a habit of attempting to ruin things like Adam Conover without actually ruining anything. In fact, innovators make things better.

Be careful not to simply challenge things for the sake of challenging them. Being mindful of the fact that what you're disrupting and who you're disrupting is key. It's about challenging convention from the right place. I once heard a pitch where someone uttered the words, "We're going to destroy the postal industry." Ouch! That's a lot of people's jobs and lives we're talking about destroying. Challenge and ask questions, but always with an eye toward affecting people's lives for the better.

LOOK AT EVERY ANGLE

When you're questioning the status quo and challenging the norm, it's important to get as many different points of view on things as possible. Adam does a great job of this on his show, examining the why of things from so many different angles. It's often when you see things through someone else's eyes that real breakthroughs happen. He'll give a history lesson, talk to a professor or expert, offer pop-up facts on the screen, and include articles and books on the topic at hand.

Maybe you've played the game where you look at something and squint your eyes so that it looks like something else. Or a game of Telephone, in which whatever you were talking about is completely ruined at the end. The best part is the discussion of where and who it went wrong with.

"I didn't say 'lab coat'! I said 'a mad goat!'"

"Who would say anything about a 'mad goat?'"

I've seen some pretty terrible bar fights break out over

games of telephone. But at the end of the day, it's about hearing and understanding multiple people and points of view and translating it into some form of your own creative output.

ALWAYS ASK "WHAT IF?"

Asking questions leads to great solutions and greater purpose. It also can help you avoid massive mistakes. I've seen this many times in my own career.

Each year, my team creates an annual trends report. At the beginning of the process, we ask everybody to submit ideas for what they think is going to be a trend in the next twelve to eighteen months. What new cultural or technology trend will take off? Which ones will crash and burn?

Two years ago, I suggested that we include marijuana in the report, and I got a lot of pushback from the team. The conventional thinking of the team was "It could be a trend, but is it really a trend in the sense of how brands interact with culture?"

"Not necessarily," I replied. "But does it always need to be spot on? There are certain things that people need to be educated about so they can extrapolate data relevant to their industries. The culture in California is about to shift because of the legalization of marijuana. How will that affect film studios or entertainment properties or snack makers?"

I was fighting stigma. In many ways, weed needs to be looked at differently as a cultural touchpoint. Let's look at the history and implications and business cases rather than our own perception and knowledge.

As much as I pushed back, I didn't win that battle. We ended up not including marijuana as a trend in the report. But from a procedural standpoint, that type of question-and-answer discussion is what I'm in the business of doing. If you want to disrupt, you should be asking, "What if?" all the time. Question everything.

That's how true innovation works. You start by asking questions, and they lead you to something that no one has ever done. We brainstormed and asked questions about something that seemed impossible—putting video ads in printed magazines. How awesome would it be for someone to flip through a magazine and suddenly find a video playing in the middle of a print magazine. That's where asking questions led us. Of course, then we had to figure out how to make it possible. It was our four-minute mile. We were the first to do it, and several have done it since.

FIND A PARADE AND GET IN FRONT OF IT

Jamen Shively, a former top executive at Microsoft, was a guest on the show. When the first wave of legalized marijuana hit, he left a "kushy" role at one of the world's top technology firms to start a luxury cannabis business, Diego Pellicer, alongside the former president of Mexico. His decision left many people scratching their heads, but Jamen was not deterred by their skepticism.

As he told me, "The best way to lead a parade is to find one and get in front of it."

At the time, there weren't very many organized entities at the forefront of the industry. He saw what was about to happen in the cannabis field, and he started questioning his own reality. He had never smoked a joint in his life, never even had an encounter with marijuana. He saw it as a disruptive business opportunity, and it attracted him. Like most innovators, Jamen saw a trend happening in the marketplace, and then he figured out a way to own it.

Some of the best innovations start with something that seems a little mundane. For a long time, marijuana was considered as a hobby for hippies. Now it's being legalized all over the US. Today it provides a different set of opportunities for people to thrive and make livelihoods for themselves.

Disruption might mean ruining things in the short term in service of something greater. For example, look at the legislation that's being worked out with Airbnb. In some cities like LA, Airbnb is free to operate. But in places like Venice and New York, it's practically illegal. Airbnb is creating disruption in the short term, but long term, it will mean we can all share and grow and become better contributors to society.

Question everything. But make sure you're working toward a greater purpose and moving society forward.

CONCLUSION

BE DUMB ENOUGH TO
DO IT ANYWAY

You may do all the stuff I've talked about in this book and not see the needle move. When that happens, it's decision time. You can give up and do something else. Or you can be dumb enough to keep doing it anyway. The path to success always lies in being naïve and dumb enough to do it anyway.

Walt Disney was told that his cartoon mouse was too scary for children. He kept doing it anyway. Stephen King was rejected by publishers and told his spooky stories would never sell. He kept doing it anyway. Henry Ford heard over and over that people wanted a faster horse, not a motorcar. He kept doing it anyway. This list of entrepreneurs and innovators who kept doing it anyway reads like a who's who of the most successful people in the world. This is one of the great keys to success. You may have to slow down or recalibrate or pivot, but regardless of what rules you've been given, continue to break them.

A TRUE INSPIRATION

Victor Pineda is a famous disability rights advocate, a dear friend and collaborator, and one of the most inspirational people I've ever met. I traveled with Victor to Kenya in 2012 doing a project with George Soros's Open Society Institute. I sat in a room for about ten days with people from all over the African continent who had disabilities. At the time, President Obama helped change the United Nations policy for how people with disabilities were treated in developing countries because many disabled people were being abused.

For example, albinos were being hunted in certain African countries. There were cases of people with polio being chained to trees because their society didn't know what to do with them. From an accessibility standpoint, people in wheelchairs couldn't get into city hall—or get around any urban development for that matter—because there was no accessibility.

Victor's story is pretty incredible. He was not disabled until he was about five years old. That's when he started experiencing all sorts of unclassified muscle failures. It got worse. So bad, in fact, that his mom moved from Venezuela to the US just to provide him with the proper opportunity to live a normal life. This was long before the Americans with Disabilities Act was passed in 1990. 1990! And America was first. A couple years ago, Victor created a documentary about himself called *12 Bends*. He has twelve bends in his body that most of us do not have—it's the way his body is. He uses a breathing machine almost twenty-four hours a day.

I once saw him interviewed by a television news anchor, and when asked to explain his condition, he made it extremely relatable. "I need a wheelchair to get around, the same way you need glasses to see. A disability is only relative to a person's environment and physical capability."

But Victor had a plan for his life, and he was determined to do it no matter what. Because his conditions were rare, there was no rulebook or set of procedures established for managing his health. He went to college, and he earned his PhD at UCLA. He was appointed by the Obama administration to be a liaison to the White House for people with disabilities. He has been to every continent and almost every country. Victor is married, he has stepchildren, and he's lived a fuller life than most of the people I know. This all took a lot of invention and imagination and teamwork and naïveté to pull off.

EXPERIENCE THE LEARNING CURVES

One of the important lessons I learned from Victor is that a challenge or a setback is only as serious as you allow it to be. You set your own limits. Victor could have set his limits very low. But instead he raised them up higher than most people would ever dare.

For a long time, my daily prayer was for capacity. I would pray for the capacity to be able to handle more, do more, and take on additional work. Seems like a crazy ask, but hear me out.

Raising your own limits and your expectations takes practice. But the more you do it, the better you'll be at doing it. It's kind of like learning to drive. When you get behind the wheel for the first time, you are very careful, you remember to keep your hands at ten and two, you check the side mirror and the rearview mirror, you remember to use your turn signal, and so on. There is so much to remember that it's almost overwhelming. But you slowly get used to it.

Eventually, driving becomes second nature. You no longer have to remember to use the turn signal. Pretty soon you're eating a cheeseburger while talking on the phone, singing in the car, dancing, and listening to *Innovation Crush*...all while dodging traffic on the highway. (This is kind of also what I imagine O.J. Simpson and Al Cowlings were doing in the white Bronco on the 405 Freeway.)

Everything that was daunting to you in the beginning is now second nature.

Allow yourself to experience the learning curves, and remember that the difficulties come from newness. When I first started learning martial arts, I didn't even know how to make a proper fist. I didn't know that you punch with your first two knuckles. Once I learned the fundamentals, I had to concentrate on what I was doing all the time. I was punching the bag and my wrist would bend, and it would hurt because I didn't have enough practice at it yet. Eventually, I moved up in rank, and it became easy. At that point, I didn't even think about it.

LIFE AND DEATH RISK

Victor literally risks his life every time he takes a trip. And he's been to over one hundred countries in his career, many of them multiple times. He owns a one-of-a-kind wheelchair that cost $100,000. There's no backup. His wheelchair was designed specifically for him. When we went to Kenya and landed in Nairobi, the airline almost sent his wheelchair through the baggage carousel, which wasn't tall enough for the wheelchair to fit.

Another guy on the trip—Nirvan Mullick, who is a unique individual himself—jumped through the carousel to the other side to stop it in the nick of time. If the wheelchair was damaged, Victor would either have been stranded in Kenya for months, or he could have even died. Talk about risk! If Nirvan had done that in an airport in other African nations, he might have wound up in prison. It's a whole team effort making sure Victor has the wheelchair he needs to travel in Kenya.

Nirvan and I had many conversations about watching Victor do what he does. It was inspiring not only to the people we worked with, but to me and everyone we came in contact with. When you see somebody doing what they want to do with no excuses, despite incredibly difficult circumstances, it makes you realize that you truly have no limits.

Victor told me he wonders if he's doing enough for the world. There's so much he wants to accomplish. The key is to keep going. Be aware of the risks, but keep going.

It's up to you to determine if you will give up or fail to achieve your goals and dreams. I've seen how Victor Pineda has overcome the most incredible challenges and setbacks, yet he is still making his mark on the world. You can, too.

ABOUT THE AUTHOR

CHRIS DENSON is an award-winning innovator, marketer, recovering comedian, and host of the *Innovation Crush* podcast, with more than seven hundred thousand subscribers worldwide. He's been featured in *Adweek*, *Forbes*, the *New York Times*, and *Inc.*, and he currently works with several Fortune 500 companies, helping them build their futures.